Exercises in Intertemporal Open-Economy Macroeconomics

Thomas H. Krueger and
Jonathan D. Ostry

The MIT Press
Cambridge, Massachusetts
London, England

This book was set in Palatino by Asco Trade Typesetting Ltd., Hong Kong, and printed and bound by in the United States of America.

ISBN 0-262-61085-X

To Cornelia and Rachel

Contents

I Prologue

1   Structure of the Book

This book is a companion volume to Frenkel's and Razin's (hereafter FR) *Fiscal Policies and the World Economy: An Intertemporal Approach*, second edition (MIT Press, 1992). It contains problems and solutions related to the material covered in FR, and the intended audience, like that of FR, consists of senior undergraduates and graduate students who are taking a course in open-economy macroeconomics.

The exercises fall into two main categories. The first consists of fairly straightforward applications of the material in FR. This type of exercise is meant to familiarize the student with the concepts and tools developed in that book. The second consists of slightly more advanced material, much of which is adapted from recently published journal articles. In this context, a selected bibliography is contained at the end of this book, and students are encouraged to consult references listed there if a problem piques their interest. The numbers in square brackets listed at the end of each section refer to selections from the bibliography that were used extensively in drawing up the problems.

The structure of the book is as follows. Part II covers the material in part II of FR, namely "Traditional Approaches to Fiscal Policies in the Open Economy." Seven problems are included here, dealing both with the income-expenditure model of chapter 2, and the Mundell-Fleming perfect-capital-mobility model of chapter 3.

Part III deals with "Elements of Intertemporal Macroeconomics," part III of FR. The first four problems illustrate the material covered in chapter 4, which is concerned with a one-good model. The second set of four problems deals with the material in chapter 5, which develops a two-tradable-good model.

Part IV of this book deals with "An Intertemporal Approach to Fiscal Policies in the World Economy," which is covered in part IV of FR. There are three problems illustrating (and extending) the material on government spending covered in chapter 6 of FR. There follow two sets of three problems, dealing respectively with budget deficits under lump-sum taxation (chapter 7 of FR) and the open-economy overlapping generations model (chapter 8 of FR).

Part V of the book deals with the material covered in part V of FR, "Distortionary Tax Incentives: Concepts and Applications." A set of three problems deals with selected aspects of distortionary taxation in an open economy, that is, the material of chapters 9 and 12 of FR. The second group of three problems covers the material in chapter 10, dealing with budget deficits under distortionary taxation. Finally, the last set of four problems relates to the material of chapter 11 on real-exchange-rate effects of fiscal policies.

The last section of the book covers material in part VI of FR. Three exercises deal with fiscal policies in a stochastic environment. The exercises illustrate the implications of uncertainty about government taxes and expenditures for private-sector consumption and portfolio choices.

In putting together this set of problems, we have drawn on some of the exercises that were given to us as graduate students at the University of Chicago and on some of the problems that we developed as teaching assistants for open-economy macro courses in subsequent years. We are also very much indebted to Professors Frenkel and Razin for their contributions to this book. Finally, we owe a great debt to the body of published research on intertemporal open-economy macroeconomics that has sprung up in the past seven or eight years. Many of the exercises in this book draw directly on published journal articles, which are cited in the selected bibliography and cross-referenced at the end of each section. Needless to say, credit for any insights provided in these exercises belongs to the original authors, and not to the authors of this book. Finally, as always, responsibility for all remaining errors is ours alone.

II

Traditional Approaches to Fiscal Policies and International Economic Interdependence

2

The Income Expenditure Model: Fiscal Policies and the Determination of Output[1]

Exercise II.2.1

Consider the fixed-price, fixed-exchange-rate, flexible-output model of chapter 2. Assume that all demand functions are such that the propensities to spend and save out of assets are the same as the propensities to spend and save out of disposable income. Assume that government spending is constant and, without loss of generality, equal to zero in all periods.

a. What is the effect on domestic and foreign output in period 0, Y_0, and Y_0^* of a unit increase in the domestic money supply, M_0, brought about by a unit decrease in domestic taxes in period 0, T_0, holding T_t constant and equal to 0, for all $t > 0$? What is the effect of this policy on the period 0 trade balance TA_0 and on the domestic money supply M_0?

b. Now consider the effect of this policy in the long run. With taxes returning to their previous value of zero and all quantities stationary over time, what is the effect on the value of domestic and foreign output in the long run? Also, how is the distribution of the world money supply affected by this policy? In answering this part of the question, you may assume that expenditure and money demand functions are linear.

Solution

Exercise II.2.1 asks us to consider the effect of a unit increase in the domestic money supply brought about by a unit decrease in T_0, and holding government spending constant. The exercise thus involves a one-shot cut in taxes, with $T_1, T_2, \ldots$, remaining unchanged. Without loss of generality, we can also assume $T_t^* = G_t^* = G_t = 0$, for all t, and $T_t = 0$, for $t > 0$. In keeping

---

1. This chapter also provides problems and solutions related to the material covered in chapter 3 of FR, "Fiscal Policies and International Capital Mobility in the Income-Expenditure Model."

with the model's Keynesian structure, it is also assumed that all prices are fixed (including the price of foreign exchange) and that they have all been normalized to unity by suitable choice of units.

a. In the short run, equilibrium in the world economy requires that world demand for each good equal the corresponding supply. Making the assumption that marginal propensities to spend and save out of disposable income are the same as the corresponding propensities to spend and save out of assets, we have the following system:

$$[(1 - s - a)/(1 - s)]Z(Y_t - T_t + M_{t-1})$$
$$+ [a^*/(1 - s^*)]Z^*(Y_t^* - T_t^* + M_{t-1}^*) = Y_t, \tag{1}$$

$$[a/(1 - s)]Z(Y_t - T_t + M_{t-1})$$
$$+ [(1 - s^* - a^*)/(1 - s^*)]Z^*(Y_t^* - T_t^* + M_{t-1}^*) = Y_t^*. \tag{2}$$

Notice that in this specification, M_{t-1} is a *predetermined* variable at time t, and therefore cannot be altered by policy. The instrument being considered here is a once-and-for-all change in T_t for $t = 0$. Totally differentiating the system of equations given by (1) and (2), we obtain

$$\begin{bmatrix} -(s + a) & a^* \\ a & -(s^* + a^*) \end{bmatrix} \begin{bmatrix} dY_0 \\ dY_0^* \end{bmatrix} = \begin{bmatrix} 1 - s - a \\ a \end{bmatrix} dT_0. \tag{3}$$

Solving the system for the two endogenous variables, and noting that $dT_0 = -1$ (since we are considering a cut in taxes by one unit), gives

$$dY_0 = [(1 - s - a)(s^* + a^*) + aa^*]/[ss^* + sa^* + as^*] > 0, \tag{4}$$

$$dY_0^* = a/[ss^* + sa^* + as^*] > 0. \tag{5}$$

Therefore, in the short run, a tax cut financed by an increase in the domestic money supply raises both domestic output and foreign output.

Having solved for the short-run effects on domestic and foreign output, it is straightforward to solve for the effects on the trade balance in period 0, TA_0. Totally differentiating the expression for the trade balance,

$$TA_t = [a^*/(1 - s^*)]Z^*(Y_t^* - T_t^* + M_{t-1}^*) - [a/(1 - s)]Z(Y_t - T_t + M_{t-1}) \tag{6}$$

gives

$$dTA_0 = a^* dY_0^* - a(dY_0 - dT_0). \tag{7}$$

Substituting from equations (4) and (5), and recalling that $dT_0 = -1$, gives

$$dTA_0 = -as^*/[ss^* + sa^* + as^*] < 0. \tag{7'}$$

Thus, the tax cut causes the trade balance to "worsen" in period 0. Notice, however, that despite the worsening of the trade balance (or equivalently, the balance of payments), the domestic money supply still rises in period 0 because of the transfer from the government. Specifically, recalling once again that the transfer (that is, the tax cut) is equal to unity, we have that

$$dM_0 = 1 - dTA_0 = [ss^* + sa^*]/[ss^* + sa^* + as^*] > 0. \tag{8}$$

b. In the long run, three conditions must be satisfied:

(i) The world money supply must be demanded by domestic and foreign residents;

(ii) Each country's private sector spending must equal disposable income;

(iii) The balance of trade must be equal to zero.

Using the notation of chapter 2 and adopting the linear versions of the spending and money demand functions, we can write these conditions as

(i) $s(Y + M) + s^*(Y^* + \overline{M} - M) = \overline{M}$,

(ii) $(1 - s)(Y + M) = Y$; $(1 - s^*)(Y^* + \overline{M} - M) = Y^*$,

(iii) $a^*(Y^* + \overline{M} - M) - a(Y + M) = 0$.

Substituting (ii) into (i) and (iii), we obtain

$$[s/(1 - s)]Y + [s^*/(1 - s^*)]Y^* = \overline{M}, \tag{8}$$

$$\bar{a}^*Y^* - \bar{a}Y = 0, \tag{9}$$

where $\bar{a}^* = a^*/(1 - s^*)$ and $\bar{a} = a/(1 - s)$. Equations (8) and (9) incorporate all the conditions that must be satisfied in long-run equilibrium. Noting that $d\overline{M} = -dT_0$, that is, the change in the world money supply is equal to minus the one-shot change in domestic taxes, we can differentiate the above system to obtain

$$\begin{bmatrix} s/(1-s) & s^*/(1-s^*) \\ -\bar{a} & \bar{a}^* \end{bmatrix} \begin{bmatrix} dY \\ dY^* \end{bmatrix} = \begin{bmatrix} -dT_0 \\ 0 \end{bmatrix}. \tag{10}$$

Solving for the endogenous variables (recalling that $dT_0 = -1$) gives

$$dY = \bar{a}^*/[s\bar{a}^*/(1 - s) + s^*\bar{a}/(1 - s^*)] > 0, \tag{11}$$

$$dY^* = \bar{a}/[s\bar{a}^*/(1 - s) + s^*\bar{a}/(1 - s^*)] > 0, \tag{12}$$

so that the long-run changes in domestic and foreign output are both positive. Finally, using the fact that under the linear specification of the spending and money demand functions, $M = [s/(1 - s)]Y$, we have that the long-run changes in the domestic and foreign money supplies are given by

$$dM = [s/(1 - s)]dY$$

$$= a^*s/(a^*s + s^*a) > 0, \tag{13}$$

$dM^* = 1 - dM$ (since the increase in the *world* money supply is one)

$$= s^*a/(a^*s + s^*a) > 0.$$

Exercise II.2.2

Consider the "dual" to the fixed-price Keynesian model of chapter 2 in which prices were fixed and output variable. Specifically, assume in this exercise that output is fixed at its full-employment level, which is normalized to unity in both countries, and that the prices of all goods are perfectly flexible. As in chapter 2, we continue to assume that the exchange rate is fixed and set equal to unity. Finally, assume as in exercise II.1.b that all behavioral functions are linear, that the domestic and foreign governments run balanced budgets in all periods, and that government spending in the foreign country is equal to zero in all periods.

a. Write down the conditions that must be satisfied in the short-run equilibrium. Also write down an expression for the nominal trade balance.

b. Solve explicitly for the (short-run) equilibrium domestic and foreign price level in terms of the level of *nominal* government spending and the world money stock. Substitute these solutions into your expression for the nominal trade balance, and obtain an expression for the latter in terms of these exogenous variables. Using the expression for the trade balance and the relation $M_t = M_{t-1} + TA_t$, show that the coefficient multiplying M_{t-1} in the equation for M_t is positive and less than unity and, hence, that the changes in the domestic money supply that occur during the process of adjustment eventually come to a halt; that is, the system converges to its long-run equilibrium.

c. Show that, if the initial level of government spending is equal to zero, then a rise in M_{t-1} (consequent on a trade balance surplus) worsens the home country's terms of trade (that is, raises P_t^*/P_t) if the sign of the parameter b is positive, where $b = a^*(s^*a - sc^*) - a(1 - s^*)(s^*c - sa^*)$.

d. Solve explicitly for the domestic and foreign price levels in the long run.

e. Show that the effect of a balanced-budget increase in government spending by the home country results in a negative comovement of domestic and foreign levels of nominal private sector spending in both the short run and the long run. Are short-run changes in nominal spending smaller or larger than the corresponding long-run changes? Why?

Solution

a. In the short run, world demand for each of the two goods must equal the available supply, viz.,

$$(1 - s - a)(P_t - G_t + M_{t-1}) + a^*(P_t^* + M_{t-1}^*) + (1 - a^g)G_t = P_t, \tag{1}$$

$$a(P_t - G_t + M_{t-1}) + (1 - s^* - a^*)(P_t^* + M_{t-1}^*) + a^g G_t = P_t^*, \tag{2}$$

and the expression for the nominal trade balance is given by

$$TA_t = a^*(P_t^* + M_{t-1}^*) - a(P_t - G_t + M_{t-1}) - a^g G_t, \tag{3}$$

where G_t now denotes government spending in nominal terms, TA_t denotes the nominal trade balance, and all other notation is as in chapter 2.

b. Equations (1) and (2) can be solved for the two endogenous variables P_t and P_t^* in terms of the parameters and exogenous variables. Recalling that $M_{t-1}^* = \overline{M} - M_{t-1}$, the system can be written in matrix form as

$$\begin{bmatrix} -(s + a) & a^* \\ a & -(s^* + a^*) \end{bmatrix} \begin{bmatrix} P_t \\ P_t^* \end{bmatrix}$$

$$= \begin{bmatrix} a^g - a - s & a^* - c & -a^* \\ -(a^g - a) & -(a - c^*) & -c^* \end{bmatrix} \begin{bmatrix} G \\ M_{t-1} \\ \overline{M} \end{bmatrix}, \tag{4}$$

which is identical to the system given in chapter 2 except that the endogenous variables are now the domestic and foreign price levels rather than the domestic and foreign output levels. This system can be solved to yield

$$P_t = [1 - s^* a^g/(ss^* + sa^* + s^* a)]G$$

$$+ [(s^* c - sa^*)M_{t-1} + a^* \overline{M}]/(ss^* + sa^* + s^* a), \tag{5}$$

$$P_t^* = [sa^g G + (s^* a - sc^*)M_{t-1} + a(1 - s^*)\overline{M}]/(ss^* + sa^* + s^* a). \tag{6}$$

Substituting equations (5) and (6) into equation (3) yields the following expression for the nominal trade balance (in terms of exogenous variables only):

$$TA_t = [-ss^*a^gG - (sa^* + s^*a)M_{t-1} + a^*s\overline{M}]/(ss^* + sa^* + s^*a). \tag{7}$$

Using equation (7) and the relation $M_t = M_{t-1} + TA_t$, we have

$$M_t = [a^*s\overline{M} - ss^*a^gG + ss^*M_{t-1}]/(ss^* + sa^* + s^*a), \tag{8}$$

with $0 < \partial M_t/\partial M_{t-1} = ss^*/(ss^* + sa^* + s^*a) < 1$ as required.

c. Assuming that $G = 0$, and dividing the expression in equation (6) by the corresponding expression in equation (5) yields the following solution for the equilibrium terms of trade:

$$P_t^*/P_t = [(s^*a - sc^*)M_{t-1} + a(1 - s^*)\overline{M}]/[(s^*c - sa^*)M_{t-1} + a^*\overline{M}]. \tag{9}$$

Differentiation of equation (9) with respect to M_{t-1} yields

$$\partial(P_t^*/P_t)/\partial M_{t-1}$$
$$= \overline{M}[a^*(s^*a - sc^*) - a(1 - s^*)(s^*c - sa^*)]/[(s^*c - sa^*)M_{t-1} + a^*\overline{M}]^2, \tag{10}$$

which is positive if and only if $b = [a^*(s^*a - sc^*) - a(1 - s^*)(s^*c - sa^*)] > 0$. This shows that a redistribution of the world money supply in favor of the home country worsens the latter's terms of trade if the parameter b is positive but improves the terms of trade if $b < 0$. Notice that the sign of b depends on differences in tastes between the domestic and foreign country. In the special case in which tastes are identical so that $s = s^*$, $a = c^*$, and $c = a^*$, b is equal to zero and redistributions of the world money supply (resulting from trade imbalances) have no effect on the equilibrium terms of trade between domestic and foreign goods.

d. The same three conditions as given in exercise II.1.b must also be satisfied here. To solve for the long-run prices, we first note that the equality of disposable income and private-sector spending in each country implies

$$(P - G + M) = 1/(1 - s)(P - G); \quad (P^* + \overline{M} - M) = 1/(1 - s^*)P^*. \tag{11}$$

Substituting equation (11) into the condition for money-market equilibrium and zero trade balance yields

$$s(P - G)/(1 - s) + s^*P^*/(1 - s^*) = \overline{M}, \tag{12}$$

$$\bar{a}^*P^* - \bar{a}P + (\bar{a} - a^g)G = 0. \tag{13}$$

Equations (12) and (13) can be solved in standard fashion for the long-run values of the domestic and foreign price levels, P and P^*, in terms of the exogenous variables G and $\overline{M}$. The solutions are

$$P = [1 - (1 - s)s^*a^g/(sa^* + s^*a)]G + [a^*(1 - s)/(sa^* + s^*a)]\overline{M}, \tag{14}$$

$$P^* = [s(1 - s^*)a^g/(sa^* + s^*a)]G + [a(1 - s^*)/(sa^* + s^*a)]\overline{M}. \tag{15}$$

e. Substituting the expression for the equilibrium price level P_t (equation 5) into the definition of nominal spending $Z_t = (1 - s)(P_t - G + M_{t-1})$, it is straightforward to show that

$$\partial Z_t/\partial G = -(1 - s)s^*a^g/(ss^* + sa^* + s^*a) < 0. \tag{16}$$

Therefore, the balanced-budget rise in G lowers nominal private spending in the short run. Similarly, substituting equation (6) into the expression for foreign nominal spending $Z_t^* = (1 - s^*)(P_t^* + \overline{M} - M_{t-1})$ reveals that

$$\partial Z_t^*/\partial G = (1 - s^*)sa^g/(ss^* + sa^* + s^*a) > 0. \tag{17}$$

Therefore, private spending rises in the foreign country and it may be concluded that, in the short run, a balanced-budget rise in government spending induces a negative comovement between domestic and foreign private nominal spending.

Substituting equations (14) and (15) into the expressions for the long-run levels of nominal spending reveals that

$$\partial Z/\partial G = -(1 - s)s^*a^g/(sa^* + s^*a) < 0, \tag{18}$$

$$\partial Z^*/\partial G = (1 - s^*)sa^g/(sa^* + s^*a) > 0. \tag{19}$$

Clearly, therefore, the balanced-budget rise in government spending results in a negative comovement between nominal spending levels in the two countries. Comparing equations (18) and (19) with equations (16) and (17) reveals that the long-run changes in spending levels exceed the corresponding short-run changes. The reason can be understood with reference to equation (7), which shows that a rise in G worsens the home-country's trade balance position. The resulting move in the balance of payments leads to a redistribution of the world money supply from the home to the foreign country, which tends to raise the spending level abroad and lower it domestically.

Exercise II.2.3

Consider the model with fixed output and flexible prices outlined in exercise II.2.2.

a. Prove that a balanced-budget increase in government spending improves the home-country's long-run terms of trade if and only if the domestic private sector's propensity to import out of spending ($\bar{a} = a/(1 - s)$) exceeds the government import propensity, a^g.

b. Define the domestic consumer price index, P_c, as a geometric weighted average of the domestic and foreign GDP deflators, P and P^*, with weights equal to the domestic expenditure shares. Thus, the weight of domestic goods in P_c would be $\bar{c} = (1 - s - a)/(1 - s)$, and the weight of foreign goods would be $\bar{a} = a/(1 - s)$, and clearly $\bar{c} + \bar{a} = 1$. Define the level of domestic and foreign real spending as nominal spending in the particular country divided by the corresponding consumer price index, that is, $E = Z/P_c$, and $E^* = Z^*/P_c^*$ where E and E^* denote real spending levels at home and abroad, respectively. Show that, from an initial position in which $G = G^* = 0$, the long-run proportional change in E^* from a balanced-budget rise in government spending originating in the domestic economy is positive if and only if $a^g < \bar{a}$. Also show that the long-run proportional change in E caused by a balanced-budget increase in G is always negative, independent of differences in the import propensities between the government and the private sector. In this last part, it is necessary to recall the restriction that $1 - s - a > 0$; that is, that the marginal propensity to consume domestic goods is positive.

Solution

a. Dividing equation (15) of exercise II.2.2 by equation (14) yields the expression for the long-run terms of trade. Differentiating that expression with respect to G yields

$$\partial(P^*/P)/\partial G = \text{constant}(a^g - \bar{a}), \tag{1}$$

where the constant is positive and is defined by

$$\text{constant} = [\overline{M}(1 - s^*)(sa^* + s^*a)(1 - s)]/$$

$$[(sa^* + s^*a - (1 - s)s^*a^g) + a^*(1 - s)\overline{M}]^2 > 0.$$

Clearly, therefore, a balanced-budget rise in G improves the long-run terms of trade of the home country (that is, lowers P^*/P) if and only if the domestic private sector's propensity to import out of spending, $\bar{a}$, exceeds the government import propensity, a^g.

b. From the definition of nominal spending and the solution for the equilibrium price level (equation 14), it is straightforward to show that

$$Z = [(1 - s)/(sa^* + s^*a)][-s^*a^gG + a^*\overline{M}].\tag{2}$$

Differentiating equation (2) logarithmically and evaluating around $G = 0$ gives

$$d\log Z/dG = -s^*a^g/a^*\overline{M}.\tag{3}$$

Recalling that, since P_c is a geometric average of P and P^* given in equations (14) and (15), the elasticities of P_c with respect to P and P^* must be the corresponding expenditure shares, we can subtract the log-differential of P_c from the expression given in equation (3) to obtain

$$d\log E/dG = (sa^* + s^*a)(\bar{a} - a^g - 1)/[a^*(1 - s)\overline{M}].\tag{4}$$

Notice that, since $\bar{a} - a^g$ is a fraction (recall that $1 - s - a > 0$), it is clear that the expression in equation (4) is necessarily negative. This means that a balanced-budget rise in G must reduce real domestic private spending in the long run, independent of any differences in tastes between the domestic public and private sectors. Proceeding in an analogous fashion for the foreign country reveals that

$$d\log E^*/dG = -(sa^* + s^*a)(\bar{a} - a^g)/[a(1 - s^*)\overline{M}].\tag{5}$$

Clearly, real foreign spending rises if the home government's import propensity exceeds the domestic private sector's import propensity, but falls otherwise. Notice that, from equation (1), this implies that foreign real spending rises when the foreign country's terms of trade improve, but falls when they deteriorate. In the case of the home country, real private spending falls in proportion to the increase in government spending when there are no terms-of-trade effects induced by differences between a^g and $\bar{a}$. Terms-of-trade effects may mitigate or reinforce the direct effects of the rise in G (which occur because of the increase in taxes needed to finance more government spending) but may never overwhelm them, as shown in equation (4).

Exercise II.2.4

Consider the fixed-exchange-rate, perfect-capital-mobility model of chapter 3. Consider the case of a small country that takes foreign demand for its output (assumed for convenience to be zero) as given and faces a given exogenous world rate of interest. Suppose that initial government spending, taxes, and debt are all zero and that, in the initial stationary equilibrium, this economy is neither a net borrower nor a net lender in world capital markets. Consider the effect of an exogenous increase in the world rate of interest.

a. What is the effect on output and the equilibrium money stock in the short run?

b. How does output behave in the long run? In signing your answer, you may assume, as in chapter 3, that a rise in income worsens the current account of the balance of payments (namely $a > r(s - M_y)$).

c. Compare your answers to a and b. Does output move in the same direction in the short run as in the long run? If so, does it move by more or less on impact than in the long run? If not, what accounts for the different behaviors of output in the short run and long run?

d. Show that, although the long-run effect on money holdings is ambiguous, a rise in the world rate of interest necessarily increases the private sector's holdings of financial assets, $M - B$, in the steady state.

Solution

a. Output in the short run is determined by the goods-market-clearing condition

$$(1 - \beta_m)E(Y_t + M_{t-1} - R_{t-1}B_{t-1}; r) = Y_t, \tag{1}$$

while the equilibrium money stock is determined, given the level of income, by the demand for money at any instant,

$$M(Y_t + M_{t-1} - R_{t-1}B_{t-1}; r) = M_t. \tag{2}$$

Differentiating equation (1), the effect on output Y_t of a rise in the world interest rate r is given by

$$dY_t/dr = [(1 - s - a)E_r]/[(1 - s)(s + a)] < 0. \tag{3}$$

Therefore, output necessarily falls in the short run. Using equation (3) and totally differentiating equation (2), we find that the money stock changes by

$$dM_t/dr = M_y[(1 - s - a)E_r]/[(1 - s)(s + a)] + M_r < 0. \tag{4}$$

In contrast to the fixed-exchange-rate model without capital mobility in which the money stock changes gradually over time through the balance of payments, the change in the money supply is instantaneous here and occurs through asset swaps (involving exchanges of money for bonds) in the world capital markets.

b. In the long run, the system determines endogenously the level of income (Y), of private-sector debt (B), and of the money stock (M). The three equilibrium conditions are: (i) income equals spending (zero saving); (ii) demand for domestically produced goods equals supply of domestically produced goods; and (iii) equality of money demand and supply:

(i) $E(Y + M - (1 + r)B; r) = Y - rB$

(ii) $(1 - \beta_m)E(Y + M - (1 + r)B; r) = Y$

(iii) $M(Y + M - (1 + r)B; r) = M.$

Totally differentiating conditions (i)–(iii) and evaluating the results around an initial steady state with $B = 0$, we obtain

$$
\begin{bmatrix}
-s & s(1 + r) - 1 & 1 - s \\
-(s + a) & -(1 + r)(1 - s - a) & 1 - s - a \\
M_y & -(1 + r)M_y & -(1 - M_y)
\end{bmatrix}
\begin{bmatrix}
dY \\
dB \\
dM
\end{bmatrix}
$$

$$
=
\begin{bmatrix}
-E_r \\
-(1 - \beta_m)E_r \\
-M_r
\end{bmatrix}
dr.
\tag{5}
$$

Recalling that $\beta_m = a/(1 - s)$, solving for the effect on output gives

$$dY/dr = -r(1 - s - a)[E_r(1 - M_y) + M_r(1 - s)]/$$
$$\{[a - r(s - M_y)](1 - s)\},
\tag{6}$$

which is positive under the assumption that an increase in income worsens the external current account balance.

c. Comparing equations (3) and (6), it is clear that output falls on impact, but rises in the long run. The intuition is as follows:
Expenditure falls on impact, and this determines the behavior of output in the short run. From equation (4), we know that on impact, agents reduce their holdings of money and increase their holdings of bonds (that is, reduce B) to take advantage of the higher return paid on these assets. In the long run, the change in the private sector's holdings of bonds is given by

$$dB/dr = a[E_r(1 - M_y) + M_r(1 - s)]/\{[a - r(s - M_y)](1 - s)\} < 0.
\tag{7}$$

With B falling in the long run, the righthand side of condition (i) above rises, but the effect of the increase in r on the lefthand side of (i) is to reduce expenditures. Thus, for a given level of output Y, income rises and expenditures fall, increasing the economy's saving level (or equivalently its current account surplus). The zero-saving condition is restored by an increase in output Y, which raises expenditures and closes the gap between income and spending.

d. Solving for the effect on money holdings from (5) gives

$$dM/dr = \{M_r[a(1-s) - rs(1-s)]$$
$$+ E_r[-M_y[a + r(1-s)]\}/\{[a - r(s - M_y)](1-s)\}, \qquad (8)$$

which cannot be signed without knowldege of the relative magnitudes of the various parameters. The intuition is that the rise in r directly lowers M, but the induced rise in Y increases M. In general, the overall effect on M cannot be signed. However, the induced rise in Y necessarily raises private financial wealth. Combining equations (7) and (8) gives

$$d(M - B)/dr = -\{E_r[(1 - M_y)a + M_y[a + r(1-s)]$$
$$+ s(1-s)rM_r\}/\{[a - r(s - M_y)](1-s)\}, \qquad (9)$$

which is unambiguously positive.

Exercise II.2.5

Consider the small-country model of chapter 3 with flexible exchange rates and capital mobility. Assume that there is no government spending, taxes, or government debt. Assume that initially, the private sector is a net debtor; that is, $B_{t-1} > 0$.

a. Compute the short-run effects on output and the exchange rate of debt forgiveness in the amount of 1 unit; that is, $dB_{t-1} = -1$.

b. Compute the effects on output in the case where the small country operates with a fixed exchange rate.

c. Suppose that export earnings, D, are approximately equal to the amount of initial debt, B; in 1990, external debt for all developing countries amounted to about $1\frac{1}{4}$ times annual export earnings, so this is a reasonable approximation. Would you expect debt forgiveness of the type analyzed in parts a and b of this question to have a larger effect on output under fixed or flexible exchange rates?

Solution

a. As in the chapter, the equilibrium conditions for the small country under flexible exchange rates are

$$(1 - \beta_m)E[Y_t + M_{t-1} - (1 + r)e_t B_{-1}; r] + e_t D^* = Y_t, \tag{1}$$

$$M[Y_t + M_{t-1} - (1 + r)e_t B_{-1}; r] = M. \tag{2}$$

Totally differentiating equations (1) and (2) and choosing units such that $e_t = 1$ initially, one obtains

$$\begin{bmatrix} -(s + a) & D^* - (1 - s - a)(1 + r)B_{t-1} \\ M_y & -M_y(1 + r)B_{t-1} \end{bmatrix} \begin{bmatrix} dY_t \\ de_t \end{bmatrix}$$

$$= \begin{bmatrix} (1 - s - a)(1 + r) \\ M_y(1 + r) \end{bmatrix} dB_{t-1}. \tag{3}$$

Solving for the effects on output and the exchange rate and setting $dB_{t-1} = -1$ gives

$$dY_t = (1 + r)D^*/[(1 + r)B_{t-1} - D^*], \tag{4}$$

$$de_t = (1 + r)/[(1 + r)B_{t-1} - D^*], \tag{5}$$

the signs of which depend on the relative magnitudes of debt plus debt service, $(1 + r)B_{t-1}$, and export earnings, D^*.

b. Under fixed exchange rates, the level of output is determined by the goods-market-clearing condition alone. Taking e_t as given in equation (1) above (and setting its value at unity by appropriate choice of units), one finds that the change in output from a unit reduction in debt under a fixed-exchange-rate regime is given by

$$dY_t = (1 - s - a)(1 + r)/(s + a) > 0. \tag{6}$$

Thus, holding constant the exchange rate, a reduction in debt increases the private sector's real resources and hence its demand for current goods. In this Keynesian model, output rises to meet the increase in demand.

c. Assuming that annual export earnings are approximately equal to the stock of debt, equation (4) shows that the change in output under flexible rates is

$$dY_t = (1 + r)/r > 0. \tag{4'}$$

Suppose that "leakages" $s + a$ are about 0.25 and that the real interest rate is about 5 percent. For these parameters, output under fixed exchange rates rises by just over three units. By contrast, under flexible exchange rates, output rises by twenty-one units. The intuition of the much larger rise in output under flexible rates is that the increase in the private sector's available resources increases the demand for money. Under fixed exchange rates, asset swaps cause the money supply to change on impact but there is no feedback to current demand which depends only on the inherited money stock, M_{t-1}. In contrast, under flexible exchange rates, the increased demand for money is offset by a depreciation of the exchange rate and the equilibrium money stock is unchanged. The higher nominal exchange rate e_t in turn raises the domestic currency value of foreign demand, $e_t D^*$, and thereby indirectly stimulates domestic production, Y_t.

Exercise II.2.6

Consider the Mundell-Fleming model of chapter 3. Compare the long-run effects of changes in the nominal supply of money for a small country with a flexible-exchange-rate regime to those of a change in the nominal exchange rate in the fixed-exchange-rate regime version of the model. Does the flexible-exchange-rate model exhibit long-run neutrality in the sense that a doubling of the money stock leads to a doubling of the exchange rate, with no change in real variables? In the case of the model with fixed exchange rates, does a doubling of the exchange rate lead to a doubling of the nominal quantity of money? Explain.

Solution

Under fixed or flexible exchange rates, the model's conditions for long-run equilibrium (assuming no government spending, taxes, or debt) are given by

$$E(Y + M - (1 + r)eB; r) = Y - reB, \tag{1}$$

$$(1 - \beta_m)E(Y + M - (1 + r)eB; r) + eD^* = Y, \tag{2}$$

$$M(Y + M - (1 + r)eB; r) = M. \tag{3}$$

Under flexible exchange rates, equations (1)–(3) solve for Y, B, and e, in terms of the exogenous variables, including M. The system in totally differentiated form is

$$
\begin{bmatrix}
-s & s(1 + r) - 1 & B[s(1 + r) - 1] \\
-(s + a) & -(1 + r)(1 - s - a) & -(1 + r)(1 - s - a)B + D^* \\
M_y & -(1 + r)M_y & -(1 + r)M_y B
\end{bmatrix}
\begin{bmatrix}
dY \\
dB \\
de
\end{bmatrix}
$$

$$
=
\begin{bmatrix}
-(1 - s) \\
-(1 - s - a) \\
1 - M_y
\end{bmatrix}
dM. \tag{4}
$$

It is clear that changes in M will indeed have effects on, for example, the real value of output, Y. Similarly, the fixed-exchange-rate version of the model in totally differentiated form is given by

$$
\begin{bmatrix}
-s & s(1+r)-1 & 1-s \\
-(s+a) & -(1+r)(1-s-a) & 1-s-a \\
M_y & -(1+r)M_y & -(1-M_y)
\end{bmatrix}
\begin{bmatrix}
dY \\
dB \\
dM
\end{bmatrix}
$$

$$
=
\begin{bmatrix}
-B[s(1+r)-1] \\
(1-s-a)(1+r)B-D^* \\
(1+r)M_y B
\end{bmatrix}
de. \tag{5}
$$

Once again, it is straightforward to verify that changes in e do indeed have real effects.

The basic reason for the real effects of M and e is the fact that domestic prices are fixed, and in particular are not necessarily related to foreign prices according to a purchasing-power-parity requirement. Suppose, in contrast to the maintained assumption of chapter 3, that in the long run, the domestic price level P is equal to the foreign price level P^* (which we normalize here at unity) times the nominal exchange rate, e; that is, $P = eP^* = e$. Then, working from the nominal spending functions corresponding to equations (1)–(3), we have

$$
Z[PY + M - (1+r)eB; r] = PY - reB, \tag{1'}
$$

$$
(1 - \beta_m)Z[PY + M - (1+r)eB; r] + eD^* = PY, \tag{2'}
$$

$$
M[PY + M - (1+r)eB; r] = M, \tag{3'}
$$

where M is the nominal money supply, eB represents the domestic currency value of foreign bonds, eD^* is the domestic currency value of foreign demand, and PY is nominal output. Using the fact that the nominal demand functions $Z(\cdot)$ and $M(\cdot)$ are linearly homogenous in nominal resources, we can rewrite equations (1')–(3') as

$$
PE[Y + M/e - (1+r)B; r] = PY - reB, \tag{1''}
$$

$$
(1 - \beta_m)PE[Y + M/e - (1+r)B; r] + eD^* = PY, \tag{2''}
$$

$$
PL[Y + M/e - (1+r)B; r] = M, \tag{3''}
$$

where L represents the demand for real money balances. We have used the fact that, because P^* is normalized to unity, the domestic price level P is equal to the nominal exchange rate e. Now dividing both sides of (1'')–(3'') by $P = e$, we obtain

$$E[Y + M/e - (1 + r)B; r] = Y - rB, \tag{1'''}$$

$$(1 - \beta_m)E[Y + M/e - (1 + r)B; r] + D^* = Y, \tag{2'''}$$

$$L[Y + M/e - (1 + r)B; r] = M/e. \tag{3'''}$$

Clearly, all nonneutralities observed in the system given by equations (4) or (5) disappear once we enforce the requirement that domestic prices move with changes in the nominal exchange rate. In this case, it is clear from the fact that M and e always appear together in the system $(1''')–(3''')$ in ratio form that a doubling of the money supply will cause the exchange rate to double, with no further effects on any of the model's other variables. Similarly, under fixed exchange rates, a devaluation will lead to an equiproportionate increase in the nominal quantity of money, but will have no effect on any other variable in the system.

Exercise II.2.7

An important simplifying assumption in the model presented in chapter 3 was that the actual current and expected future values of the exchange rate would always be equal to one another (static expectations). Suppose, in contrast, that people do not necessarily expect the exchange rate to remain constant at its current level. If we denote by e_t^a the anticipated or expected future value of the exchange rate, then the assumption that domestic and foreign assets are identical in all respects except for currency denomination implies that the following arbitrage condition holds at all times:

$$(1 + i_t) = (e_t^a/e_t)(1 + i_t^*), \tag{1}$$

where i_t and i_t^* are the domestic and foreign nominal interest rates at time t. Under the fixed-price assumption of chapter 3, the same arbitrage condition also holds with respect to real interest rates so that

$$(1 + r_t) = (e_t^a/e_t)(1 + r_t^*). \tag{1'}$$

a. Consider the effects of a debt-financed increase in government spending on domestic goods under the assumption of fixed exchange rates, so that anticipated and actual exchange rates are always equal to one another (and may be assumed equal to unity). Assume that the country undertaking the fiscal expansion is small in world markets, that in the initial steady state the country is neither a net lender nor a net borrower in world capital markets, and that the effects of interest-rate changes on domestic absorption are negligible so that the partial derivative, E_r, of the expenditure function with respect to the domestic interest rate is zero. Consider only the short-run effects.

b. Consider now the same policy experiment under flexible exchange rates, under the assumption that the expected future exchange rate is constant. Is the effect on output larger or smaller than under fixed exchange rates?

c. Suppose now that the increase in government spending lasts for some time and that the expected exchange rate moves in the same direction as the actual exchange rate moved in part b. Is the rise in output larger or smaller than in b? If the expected exchange rate moves by the same proportion as the actual exchange rate, by how much does output change in response to the fiscal expansion?

Solution

a. Under fixed exchange rates, the market-clearing condition for domestic goods alone determines the equilibrium level of ouptut. Under the assumption that expenditure does not depend on the interest rate, we have

$$(1 - \beta_m)E(Y_t + A_{t-1}) + G + D^* = Y_t, \tag{2}$$

where we have assumed that taxes are initially zero, that all government spending is devoted to domestically produced goods, and that the fixed exchange rate e_t is initially equal to unity. Differentiation of equation (2) gives

$$dY_t/dG = 1/(s + a) \tag{3}$$

as the short-run effect on output of a debt-financed increase in government spending on domestic goods under fixed exchange rates.

b. Under flexible exchange rates, the goods and money-market equilibrium conditions jointly determine the short-run effects of fiscal policy on the level of output and the exchange rate. Substituting the interest parity condition (equation 1′) into the money demand equation, the system may be written as

$$(1 - \beta_m)E(Y_t + A_{t-1}) + G + e_t D^* = Y_t, \tag{4}$$

$$M(Y_t + A_{t-1}; (e_t^a/e_t)(1 + r^*) - 1) = M, \tag{5}$$

where we have assumed that the foreign real-interest rate is fixed, in keeping with the small-country assumption. Under the assumption that the inherited stock of debt B_{t-1} is zero, the totally differentiated version of the system given by equations (4) and (5) may be written as

$$\begin{bmatrix} -(s+a) & D^* \\ M_y & -M_r(1+r) \end{bmatrix}\begin{bmatrix} dY_t \\ de_t \end{bmatrix} = \begin{bmatrix} -1 & 0 \\ 0 & -M_r(1+r) \end{bmatrix}\begin{bmatrix} dG \\ de_t^a \end{bmatrix} \quad (6)$$

where it has been assumed that in the initial equilibrium $e_t^a = e_t = 1$. Under the assumption of the question, $de_t^a = 0$, and one can solve for the effects on output of the increase in government spending:

$$dY_t/dG = M_r(1+r)/[M_r(1+r)(s+a) - M_yD^*] > 0$$

$$= \{(s+a) - M_yD^*/[M_r(1+r)]\}^{-1} < (s+a)^{-1}. \quad (7)$$

The first line of equation (7) shows that a debt-financed increase in government spending increases output in the short run. The second line compares the effect under flexible exchange rates with the effect under fixed exchange rates, where the latter is given by the second term in the second line of equation (7), $1/(s+a)$ (see equation 3). Clearly, fiscal policy has a smaller expansionary effect under flexible exchange rates than under fixed exchange rates. The intuition is provided by focusing on the exchange-rate effects of a rise in government spending in this case, which are given by

$$de_t/dG = M_y/[M_r(1+r)(s+a) - M_yD^*] < 0. \quad (8)$$

Equation (8) shows that the rise in government spending contributes to an appreciation of the domestic currency. The latter causes a reduction in the domestic currency value of exports, which offsets part of the increase in output generated by the rise in government spending. Thus, relative to the fixed-exchange-rate case, output rises by a smaller amount in response to a debt-financed increase in government spending.

c. From the interest-parity condition, it is clear that an expected future appreciation of the currency (a fall in e_t^a) exerts an impact on the domestic interest rate opposite to that of an actual appreciation in the current period (a fall in e_t). Thus if, in response to a permanent rise in government spending, e_t^a is revised downwards, this will tend to increase the demand for money. For a given supply of money, it follows that equilibrium in the money market can only be sustained at a lower level of income. Thus, one would expect the rise in income to be smaller when the expected exchange rate adjusts than when it does not. This can be established by solving for the effect on income of a change in e_t^a (using equation 6) which is given by

$$dY_t/de_t^a = D^*M_r(1+r)/[M_r(1+r)(s+a) - M_yD^*] > 0. \quad (9)$$

Clearly, therefore, an expected appreciation (a fall in e_t^a) contributes to a fall in domestic output. It follows from the discussion above that if expected and actual exchange rates move in the same proportion in response to a permanent rise in government spending, so that the domestic interest rate is unchanged (equation 1'), then money-market equilibrium (equation 5) requires that the domestic level of output is also unchanged as a result of the rise in government spending. Thus, we have shown so far that, under the assumptions of this question, fiscal policy exerts a smaller effect on domestic output under flexible exchange rates than under fixed rates. Further, we have shown that the output effects of government spending decrease as agents revise their expectations of the future level of the exchange rate. If the expected and actual exchange rates appreciate by similar amounts in response to the change in government spending, fiscal policy has no effect at all on the level of output in a small country under flexible exchange rates.

References for Part II: [18], [19].

---

3 Fiscal Policies and International Capital Mobility in the Income-Expenditure Model

Problems and solutions related to the material of this chapter of FR were covered in the previous chapter.

III

Elements of Intertemporal Macroeconomics

4

The Composite-Commodity World

Exercise III.4.1

Consider the small open-economy model of chapter 4 in which there is a single aggregate tradable commodity. Agents receive endowments of this good in each period. For simplicity assume that the investment technology is such that it is never profitable to augment the endowment through investment. Consumers face an exogenous world discount factor, which we denote here by $R = 1/(1 + r)$ where r is the world interest rate prevailing between the two periods. For simplicity, we assume that there is no historically given debt commitment so that initial trade and current account balances are equal. The utility function of the representative consumer is taken to be

$$U = [C_1^{1-1/\sigma} + DC_2^{1-1/\sigma}]/(1 - 1/\sigma),$$

where C_t denotes consumption in period t, D is the subjective discount factor, and σ is a positive parameter. The budget constraint of the consumer is:

$$C_1 + RC_2 = Y_1 + RY_2 \equiv W$$

where Y_t denotes the endowment in period t and W is the present value of the endowment stream or wealth.

a. Determine the levels of C_1 and C_2 that maximize utility subject to the budget constraint.

b. Suppose the endowment in period 1 falls and the endowment in period 2 rises in such a way that W is unchanged. Find the effect on the current account balance between periods 1 and 2.

c. Suppose now the endowment in period 1 falls with no change in the endowment in period 2. Find the effect on the current account balance. How does it compare to your finding in part b?

d. Suppose there is an exogenous change in the world discount factor, R. Find the effect of such a change on the current account balance. What role does the parameter σ play in your answer? You may assume, in this part of the question, that the world discount factor, R, and the subjective discount factor, D, are equal in the initial equilibrium, and that the endowment is constant over time.

Solution

a. The necessary conditions for a maximum are

$$C_1^{-1/\sigma} = \lambda,$$

$$DC_2^{-1/\sigma} = \lambda R,$$

$$C_1 + RC_2 = W,$$

where λ is a Lagrange multiplier. Solving in the usual way gives

$$C_1 = \frac{W(R/D)^\sigma}{R + (R/D)^\sigma}, \tag{1}$$

$$C_2 = \frac{W}{R + (R/D)^\sigma}. \tag{2}$$

b. The current account in period 1 is given by

$$CA = Y_1 - C_1. \tag{3}$$

Since from (1), C_1 is unchanged for a supply shock that leaves wealth unchanged, it follows that $dCA/dY_1 = 1$ in this case. The interpretation is that the nature of the supply shock in this example is that income falls today but rises by an equal (in present value terms) amount tomorrow; that is, the supply shock does not change the consumer's lifetime resources. Since the consumer has free access to the world capital market, she chooses a path of consumption that depends only on her wealth level rather than on the profile of income. Since wealth is unchanged, so too is the chosen level of consumption. With current income falling, however, the agent must borrow the full amount of the income shortfall (repaying both principal and interest in the second period out of the increase in resources that is received then). The counterpart of this borrowing is a current account deficit.

c. In this case, consumption will adjust since the supply shock does not leave wealth unchanged. Differentiating equation (1) and noting that the change in wealth is equal to the change in the first-period endowment gives

$$dC_1/dY_1 = \frac{(R/D)^\sigma}{R + (R/D)^\sigma}. \tag{4}$$

The expression on the righthand side of (4) is a positive fraction implying that, in response to a transitory decline in real income, consumption adjusts less than one-for-one. Again, the means by which agents smooth their consumption stream relative to their income stream is by borrowing in the international capital market. The counterpart to this borrowing is a current account deficit which, upon differentiating (3), changes according to

$$dCA_1/dY_1 = 1 - \frac{(R/D)^\sigma}{R + (R/D)^\sigma}$$

$$= \frac{R}{R + (R/D)^\sigma}. \tag{5}$$

Clearly, therefore, a temporary negative supply shock $dY_1 < 0$ induces a current account deficit. The deficit, however, is smaller than in part b (since the expression in the second line of equation 5 is a positive fraction), reflecting the fact that consumption declines in proportion to the reduction in lifetime wealth.

d. From (3), the change in the current account is equal to minus the change in consumption, since the endowment is assumed constant in this part of the exercise. From the budget constraint, the change in the world discount factor affects wealth according to

$$dW/dR = Y_2. \tag{6}$$

Using (6) in the differentiated version of (1) and evaluating results around an initial equilibrium with $R = D$ and $Y_1 = Y_2 = Y$ gives

$$dC_1/dR = -dCA/dR = \sigma Y/(1 + R). \tag{7}$$

An increase in R, that is, a fall in world interest rates, raises consumption by an amount that depends positively on the parameter σ, which measures the elasticity of substitution between consumption in periods 1 and 2. Since the endowment is unaffected by the change in R, the deterioration in the current account resulting from the rise in consumption also depends positively on σ.

Exercise III.4.2

Consider a small open economy with preferences as described in the previous exercise, and with a positive endowment in the second period only and no endowment in period 1. As before, assume this economy has free access to the world capital market and faces a given world discount factor which is taken to be equal to the subjective discount factor in the initial equilibrium. Assume also that there is no investment or historically given debt commitment.

a. Write down the expression for the current account deficit in period 1.

b. The government decides to impose a (small) tax on international borrowing, that is, on all loans taken out in period 1 for repayment in period 2. For simplicity, assume that the interest rate inclusive of the tax on borrowing is r, with associated discount factor R, while the world interest rate is r^* with corresponding discount factor R^*. Assume that any revenue collected as a result of this tax is redistributed to private agents in a lump-sum fashion. Also assume that in the initial equilibrium $R = R^* = D$. What is the budget constraint faced by the representative consumer in this case?

c. What is the effect of the tax on foreign borrowing on the current account balance?

Solution

a. From equations (1) and (3) of the previous exercise and the fact that the agent only receives an endowment in the second period, we have

$$CA = -C_1 = \frac{-R^* Y_2 (R^*/D)}{(R^* + (R^*/D)^\sigma}. \tag{1}$$

Clearly, therefore, the economy runs a current account deficit in period 1.

b. The budget constraint faced by the representative consumer is

$$C_1 + R C_2 = R Y_2 + \text{transfer}, \tag{2}$$

where transfer indicates the redistributed revenues from the tax on foreign borrowing, which the consumer takes as given. From the budget constraint of the government, however, the transfer must be identically equal to $(r - r^*)C_1$, which is the product of the tax rate $(r - r^*)$ and the tax base C_1 (which equals borrowing in period 1 since there is no endowment in that period). Noting that this revenue, and hence the associated transfer, is only received in the second period and therefore that, on the righthand side of equation (2), the transfer must be expressed in present-value terms, we can rewrite the budget constraint as

$$C_1 + RC_2 = RY_2 + (1 - R/R^*)C_1 \equiv W, \tag{2'}$$

where we have used the fact that $r = (1 - R)/R$, and correspondingly for r^*.

c. Differentiating equation (1) and using the fact that, under the assumption that $R^* = D$, consumption is constant initially, that is, $C_1 = C_2$ in the initial equilibrium, we have

$$dCA/dR = -\sigma R^* Y_2/(1 + R^*)^2. \tag{3}$$

Since a small tax on borrowing raises r and therefore lowers $R = (1 - r)^{-1}$, equation (3) shows that the imposition of such a tax necessarily improves the current account. Moreover, as in the previous exercise, the magnitude of the current account improvement depends positively on the intertemporal elasticity of substitution, σ.

Exercise III.4.3

Consider the two-country version of the model outlined in exercise III.4.1. The representative consumer in the home country has preferences

$$U = [C_1^{1-1/\sigma} + DC_2^{1-1/\sigma}]/(1 - 1/\sigma),$$

while the consumer in the foreign country has the corresponding utility function

$$U^* = [C_1^{*1-1/\sigma^*} + D^* C_2^{*1-1/\sigma^*}]/(1 - 1/\sigma^*),$$

where a superscripted asterisk denotes a foreign economy variable, and all other notation is as in exercise III.4.1. As before, agents in each country receive endowments of the single aggregate consumption good in each period and we assume that there is no investment. There are no impediments to trade in goods or capital, and to simplify we assume no historical debt commitment. Initially, we assume that the subjective discount factors, D and D^*, are equal to one another. From the argument presented in chapter 4, the common value of the subjective discount factor must also be equal to the equilibrium world discount factor, which we denote as before by R. Finally, for the purpose of evaluating comparative statics results in the remainder of this exercise, it may be assumed that initially the profile of output (endowments) is flat in each country; that is, $Y_1 = Y_2$ and $Y_1^* = Y_2^*$.

a. What is the effect on the world discount factor, R, of an increase in world output in period 1, $Y_1 + Y_1^*$? How does an increase in world output in the second period affect R? Prove that an increase in the growth rate raises the equilibrium interest rate. What role does intertemporal substitution play in your answer?

b. Suppose output both at home and abroad grows by a given percentage in period 1. How does this affect the home country's current account position in period 1? Provide a condition involving the relative magnitudes of σ and σ^* under which the home country's current account necessarily improves.

Solution

The levels of wealth in the two countries are given by

$$W = Y_1 + RY_2, \tag{1a}$$

$$W^* = Y_1^* + RY_2^*, \tag{1b}$$

and it follows from the fact that the utility function is the same as in exercise III.4.1 that the demand functions are given by

$$C_1 = \frac{W(R/D)^\sigma}{R + (R/D)^\sigma}, \tag{2a}$$

$$C_2 = \frac{W}{R + (R/D)^\sigma}, \tag{2b}$$

$$C_1^* = \frac{W^*(R/D)^{\sigma^*}}{R + (R/D)^{\sigma^*}}, \tag{3a}$$

$$C_2^* = \frac{W^*}{R + (R/D)^{\sigma^*}}. \tag{3b}$$

The equilibrium conditions require that world supply equal world demand for goods in each of the two periods. By Walras' law, however, one of the two equilibrium conditions may be ignored. We choose to consider the market-clearing condition in the first period, namely

$$C_1 + C_1^* = Y_1 + Y_1^*. \tag{4}$$

Substituting equations (1a)–(3b) into (4) gives

$$\frac{(Y_1 + RY_2)(R/D)^\sigma}{R + (R/D)^\sigma} + \frac{(Y_1^* + RY_2^*)(R/D)^{\sigma^*}}{R + (R/D)^{\sigma^*}} = Y_1 + Y_1^*. \tag{4'}$$

Given that the endowments are exogenous, the only unknown in equation (4') is the world discount factor R. Totally differentiating (4') allows one to solve for the effects of changes in world output in each of the two periods on R

$$dR = \frac{R}{\sigma Y + \sigma^* Y^*} dY_1^w - \frac{R}{\sigma Y + \sigma^* Y^*} dY_2^w, \tag{5}$$

where the superscript ^{w} denotes world output and where we have used the assumption that in the initial equilibrium there is no output growth (so that Y is the initial level of output in the home country and Y^* is the corresponding foreign output level). Clearly, an increase in output in the current period raises R (lowers the interest rate), and the converse is true for an increase in output in the future period. The intuition is simply that a transitory increase in current output creates an excess supply of current goods relative to future goods. To clear world markets, the relative price of current goods (effectively, the real interest rate) must fall. The decline in the world interest rate reallocates demands from the future to the current period until equilibrium is restored. The economics of an increase in future output is completely symmetric to the one given here for an increase in current output.

Rearranging equation (5) gives

$$dr = \frac{R^2}{\sigma Y + \sigma^* Y^*} d\log(Y_2^w/Y_1^w), \tag{5'}$$

which shows clearly that the equilibrium interest rate is increasing in the growth rate of world output. Notice further that, for a given level of output growth, the magnitude of the required increase in the interest rate is decreasing in both the domestic and foreign elasticities of intertemporal substitution. The reason is simply that, for a given amount of excess supply in the future relative to the present (that is, a given growth rate), agents can more easily be induced to postpone consumption if present and future consumption are good substitutes; that is, if σ and σ^* are large. In this case, the required increase in the interest rate will be small. If, in contrast, present and future consumption are poor substitutes, then a relatively large rise in the interest rate is required to induce consumers to postpone consumption in line with the higher rate of growth of output.

b. Substituting equations (1a) and (2a) into the definition of the current account gives

$$CA = Y_1 - \frac{(Y_1 + RY_2)(R/D)^\sigma}{R + (R/D)^\sigma}. \tag{6}$$

We are asked to determine the effect on CA of a supply shock that affects both countries symmetrically, so that $d \log Y_1 = d \log Y_1^*$. Differentiating equation (6) and substituting (5) gives

$$dCA/d \log Y_1 = \frac{RYY^*}{(1 + R)(\sigma Y + \sigma^* Y^*)}(\sigma^* - \sigma), \tag{7}$$

where as before $Y(Y^*)$ denotes the (assumed-to-be-constant) initial level of output in the home (foreign) country. Clearly, therefore, an expansion of world output has an ambiguous effect on the current account position, which depends on the relative magnitudes of the domestic and foreign intertemporal elasticities of substitution. The intuition is as follows: Suppose agents in the home country find it difficult to substitute present for future consumption; that is, $\sigma < \sigma^*$. In this case, the fall in the world interest rate (see equation 5) induced by the transitory increase in world output has a relatively small impact on domestic consumption and a relatively large impact on foreign consumption. With domestic consumption rising by only a small amount (relative, that is, to the rise in domestic output and also relative to the increase in foreign consumption), the home country's current account moves into surplus. Conversely, if domestic consumption is highly responsive to changes in the intertemporal relative price, so that $\sigma > \sigma^*$, the relatively large increase in domestic consumption (relative, that is, to the given proportional increase in domestic or foreign output and also to the increase in foreign consumption) ensures that the home country runs a current account deficit during the period in which world output is expanding.

Exercise III.4.4

Consider the setup of the previous exercise. The utility functions of the representative agents in each country are, respectively,

$$U = [C_1^{1-1/\sigma} + DC_2^{1-1/\sigma}]/(1 - 1/\sigma),$$

$$U^* = [C_1^{*1-1/\sigma^*} + D^* C_2^{*1-1/\sigma^*}]/(1 - 1/\sigma^*),$$

with notation as described previously. In addition, it is assumed that the government in each country purchases goods and finances its expenditures via lump-sum taxation.

a. Write down the budget constraint of the representative consumer and the government in each country.

b. Under the same simplifying assumptions as followed in the previous exercise (no output growth, and subjective and world discount factors initially equal), find the effect of a transitory increase in government spending on the world discount factor. What is the effect of an anticipated future increase in government spending? Compare your answer to the one obtained in part a of the previous exercise. What is the intuition?

c. Suppose government spending is initially the same fraction of GDP in each economy and identical across periods. Suppose governments in both countries undertake a coordinated fiscal expansion whereby they raise their expenditures in proportion to GDP by the same amount in period 1 only. Will the impact of such a policy be neutral insofar as the current account is concerned? What assumptions on the behavioral parameters would ensure that the current account neither worsens nor improves as a result of such a policy?

Solution

a. The budget constraint faced by the domestic private sector is

$$C_1 + RC_2 = Y_1 + RY_2 - T_1 - RT_2 \equiv W, \tag{1}$$

where T_t denotes taxes in period t. The government's budget constraint is

$$G_1 + RG_2 = T_1 + RT_2, \tag{2}$$

where G_t denotes government spending in period t. Substituting (2) in (1) gives the effective constraint of the private sector

$$C_1 + RC_2 = Y_1 + RY_2 - G_1 - RG_2 \equiv W. \tag{3}$$

Proceeding in the same fashion for the foreign country gives the private sector's effective constraint there as

$$C_1^* + RC_2^* = Y_1^* + RY_2^* - G_1^* - RG_2^* \equiv W^*, \tag{4}$$

where, as before, a superscripted asterisk denotes a foreign-economy variable.

b. The equilibrium condition in period 1 (as before Walras's law allows us to ignore the corresponding condition for period 2) is

$$\frac{(Y_1 + RY_2 - G_1 - RG_2)(R/D)^\sigma}{R + (R/D)^\sigma} + \frac{(Y_1^* + RY_2^* - G_1^* - RG_2^*)(R/D)^{\sigma^*}}{R + (R/D)^{\sigma^*}}$$

$$= Y_1 + Y_1^* - G_1 - G_1^*, \tag{5}$$

where we have used the form of the demand function taken from the previous exercise but have incorporated the appropriate definition of real wealth. Equation (5) is instructive and may be directly compared with equation (4') of exercise III.4.3. Doing so reveals that an increase in government spending must affect the equilibrium discount factor R (the only endogenous variable in equation 5) in exactly the same manner as a negative supply shock in period 1. Similarly, an increase in government spending in period 2 must affect R in precisely the same way as an anticipated reduction in world output in that period. The intuition is simply that, in this type of model, increases in government spending have no other effect than to reduce the amount of resources available for private consumption. This "Ricardian" feature of the model ensures that government spending shocks behave exactly like supply shocks. Totally differentiating (5) gives

$$dR = -\frac{R}{\sigma Y + \sigma^* Y^*}(dG_1 + dG_1^*) + \frac{R}{\sigma Y + \sigma^* Y^*}(dG_2 + dG_2^*), \tag{6}$$

where it is clear that increases in the level of world government spending operate in precisely the same fashion as reductions in the level of world output (see equation 5 of the previous exercise).

c. Since negative supply shocks and fiscal expansions are completely symmetric insofar as their effects on world interest rates are concerned, we should also expect this symmetry to carry over to the current account effects. In fact this is the case. By definition, the current account is equal to

$$CA = Y_1 - C_1 - G_1. \tag{7}$$

Totally differentiating equation (7) and using (6) gives

$$\frac{dCA}{dG_1}\bigg|_{dG_1^* = \frac{Y_1^*}{Y_1}dG_1} = \frac{RYY^*}{(1 + R)(\sigma Y + \sigma^* Y^*)}(\sigma - \sigma^*), \tag{8}$$

where the expression following the vertical bar indicates that we are assuming that the increase in government spending is the same fraction of GDP in both countries. Clearly, whether the coordinated fiscal expansion is neutral or not depends on whether the intertemporal elasticities of substitution differ across the two countries. If consumptions in the two periods are closer substitutes at home than abroad, the rise in the interest rate associated with the temporary fiscal expansion will cause consumption to be reduced by a relatively large amount at home, thereby contributing to a current account surplus. Conversely, if $\sigma < \sigma^*$, then consumption falls by only a small amount in response to the higher interest rate, thereby inducing a current account deficit in the home country. Only in the special case in which $\sigma = \sigma^*$ will the coordinated fiscal expansion be neutral in terms of its current account effects. In this particular case, the higher interest rate induces similar reductions in consumption in both countries, implying that the current account position need not change.

5   The Multiple-Good
        World

Exercise III.5.1

Consider a simplified version of the model of chapter 5 in which there is no domestic endowment of the importable good and no domestic consumption of the exportable good. Agents receive a constant endowment Y of the exportable good in each period, which is sold in world markets at a constant price equal to unity. The import good is also purchased in world markets at a constant world price of unity. Agents can borrow and lend in world capital markets at a constant world interest rate equal to the domestic rate of time preference; the common value of the subjective and world discount factors is denoted by D. Agents have logarithmic utility given by

$$U = \log C_0 + D \log C_1 \tag{1}$$

where C_t denotes consumption of importables in period $t = 0, 1$.

a. Consider an initial equilibrium in which there is in place a constant ad valorem tariff at rate $t > 0$ levied on imports. Moreover, assume that the government rebates any collected tariff revenues in a lump-sum fashion and there is no government consumption. Compare the utility level enjoyed by the representative agent in this case to a situation in which there is free trade; that is, $t = 0$ in both periods. Note that this is not a comparative statics exercise: You are not asked to compute the effects on utility of small tariff changes; rather, you need to solve for the utility level associated with a strictly positive tariff and the utility level associated with free trade. Explain the intuition of your answer.

b. Consider the situation with a strictly positive tariff t in both periods. The government decides to lower the tariff to zero in period 0 and maintain the same level t in period 1. Is the representative consumer better or worse off than when there is a constant tariff at rate t in both periods? (Note again this is not a comparative statics exercise.) Provide an intuitive explanation for the effect of a temporary liberalization on welfare.

Solution

a. The budget constraint of the consumer is

$$(1 + t_0)C_0 + (1 + t_1)DC_1 = Y_0 + DY_1 + G_0 + DG_1 \equiv W \tag{1}$$

where G_t denotes government transfers (the rebated tariff revenue). Maximizing utility subject to the budget constraint and solving for the demands gives

$$C_0 = W/[(1 + D)(1 + t_0)], \tag{2a}$$

$$C_1 = W/[(1 + D)(1 + t_1)]. \tag{2b}$$

It is immediately obvious from (2a) and (2b) that if $t_0 = t_1 = t$, that is, the tariff rate is constant, then so too will consumption be constant, that is, $C_0 = C_1$. Now from the budget constraint of the government, we know that

$$G_0 = t_0 C_0, \tag{3a}$$

$$G_1 = t_1 C_1. \tag{3b}$$

Substituting (3a) and (3b) into (2a) and (2b) allows one to solve for C_0 and C_1 in terms of exogenous variables only. This gives[1]

$$C_0 = Y(1 + D)(1 + t_1)/(1 + D + Dt_0 + t_1), \tag{4a}$$

$$C_1 = Y(1 + D)(1 + t_0)/(1 + D + Dt_0 + t_1). \tag{4b}$$

Now suppose that $t_0 = t_1 = t$ as required in the question. Then it is straightforward to see that $C_0 = C_1 = Y$. Thus, with a constant tariff, consumption is constant and equal to the value of permanent income Y. Now consider a situation of free trade with $t_0 = t_1 = 0$. Plugging this value into equations (4a) and (4b) yields immediately that consumption is constant and equal to permanent income Y also. Since the levels of consumption are the same under free trade and with a constant tariff rate t, it follows that the utility enjoyed under both regimes is identical. In fact, plugging the values of consumption into the utility function yields that utility is in both cases equal to

---

1. We have used the assumption that the endowment of exportables is constant here.

$$U = (1 + D)\log Y. \tag{5}$$

The intuition of this result is as follows: In the model as presented above, there are no static gains from trade. This is because with one good on the consumption side, driving a wedge between the domestic and world relative prices of imports does not lead to underconsumption of imports; in fact, the tariff operates just like a lump-sum tax in this model and consequently its level has no effect on welfare. Note that this implies that the regime with a positive tariff in both periods is still a "first best" world; as a further check on this, consider the effect on welfare of raising the tariff by a small amount in period 0. You should find that, to first order, utility is unaffected by this policy.

b. Consider now the case when the tariff is equal to zero in period 0 (free trade) but positive at the same level t in period 1. In this case, equations (4a) and (4b) become

$$C_0 = Y(1 + D)(1 + t_1)/(1 + D + t_1), \tag{5a}$$

$$C_1 = Y(1 + D)/(1 + D + t_1). \tag{5b}$$

Clearly, we have $C_0 > Y$ and $C_1 < Y$, so the country consumes more in period 0 than in the flat tariff case and less in period 1. Since we saw previously that the flat tariff case was optimal (it gave the same welfare as free trade which is optimal here since the country has no monopoly power in trade) and that with a flat tariff consumption was constant through time, it follows immediately that the nonconstant path of consumption in this case must reduce welfare. In fact, this can be rigorously shown by plugging equations (5a) and (5b) into the utility function to give

$$U = (1 + D)\log Y + \log\left[\frac{(1 + D)^{(1+D)}(1 + t)}{(1 + D + t)^{(1+D)}}\right]. \tag{6}$$

The first term on the RHS of equation (6) is the utility level enjoyed in the constant tariff case. The second term is clearly equal to zero when $t = 0$ (that is, the expression inside the log sign is equal to unity). In fact this expression can be shown to be decreasing in t so that for any strictly positive tariff in period 1, utility is lower than in the constant tariff case.

The intuition is straightforward. With a zero tariff in period 0 and a positive tariff in period 1, there is an intertemporal distortion in this economy. The reason is that the world rate of interest differs from the domestic consumption rate of interest owing to the nonconstant path of the tariff. This distortion leads to overconsumption in period 0 and underconsumption in period 1, which reduces the level of utility relative to the constant tariff case. This is an interesting result because it shows that a policy of liberalizing trade flows temporarily (for example, because the government cannot credibly commit to liberalizing them permanently) may carry substantial welfare costs. One has to be cautious here, however, because the model was rigged to give this result in the sense that there was no static welfare gain to be derived from moving to free trade in period 0. If this gain were substantial, it could offset part of the loss from creating an intertemporal distortion. Nevertheless, the sharp movements in consumption (particularly consumption of durable goods imported from abroad) associated with temporary liberalization episodes (for example in some Latin American countries) have led some observers to believe that the welfare costs associated with such policies might be large.

Exercise III.5.2

Consider the model of chapter 5 in which agents consume importables and exportables and receive endowments of importables and exportables in each period. Assume that there is no investment and that world prices are constant and for convenience equal to unity in each period. Assume that the world interest rate is equal to the domestic rate of time preference, and denote the common value of the world discount factor and subjective discount factor by D. Utility is assumed to be a logarithmic function of present and future consumption indices where the latter are themselves Cobb-Douglas functions of importables and exportables consumption in each period;

$$U = \log[c_{x0}^b c_{m0}^{1-b}] + D\log[c_{x1}^b c_{m1}^{1-b}],\tag{1}$$

where $0 < b < 1$.

Consider an initial equilibrium of free trade. Determine the effects on the trade balance measured in constant world prices of the following policies:

(i) a temporary export tax imposed in period 0;

(ii) a temporary import tariff imposed in period 0;

(iii) a permanent export tax;

(iv) a permanent import tariff.

Assume in all cases that revenues from tax collections are rebated to consumers in a lump-sum fashion and that there is no government consumption.

Are any of these policies equivalent? Lerner's symmetry theorem states that import and export taxes are equivalent policies. Is this theorem valid here?

Solution

The budget constraint of the consumer is

$$c_{x0}(1 - T_0) + c_{m0}(1 + t_0) + Dc_{x1}(1 - T_1) + Dc_{m1}(1 + t_1)$$

$$= Y_{x0}(1 - T_0) + Y_{m0}(1 + t_0) + DY_{x1}(1 - T_1) + DY_{m1}(1 + t_1)$$

$$+ G_0 + DG_1 \equiv W, \tag{2}$$

where T_i is the export tax in period i and t_i is the import tariff in period i. We can also define the trade balance measured in constant world prices as

$$TA_0 = Y_{x0} + Y_{m0} - c_{x0} - c_{m0}, \tag{3}$$

where we have used the assumption that world prices are constant and assumed equal to unity. Solving in the usual way for the demand functions gives

$$c_{x0} = bW/[(1 - T_0)(1 + D)], \tag{4a}$$

$$c_{m0} = (1 - b)W/[(1 + t_0)(1 + D)], \tag{4b}$$

$$c_{x1} = bW/[(1 - T_1)(1 + D)], \tag{4c}$$

$$c_{m1} = (1 - b)W/[(1 + t_1)(1 + D)]. \tag{4d}$$

Totally differentiating the expression for the trade balance gives

$$dTA_0 = -dc_{x0} - dc_{m0}, \tag{5}$$

which upon substitution of the total differentials of equations (4a) and (4b) (taking into account the definition of W given in equation 2) gives

$$dTA_0 = -[DbW/(1 + D)^2](dT_0 - dT_1)$$

$$+ [D(1 - b)W/(1 + D)^2](dt_0 - dt_1). \tag{5'}$$

A temporary export tax is defined as $dT_0 > 0$ with $dT_1 = 0$, and a temporary import tariff is defined as $dt_0 > 0$ with $dt_1 = 0$. A permanent export tax is defined as $dT_0 = dT_1 = dT$, and a permanent import tariff as $dt_0 = dt_1 = dt$. Therefore, we have the following results:

(i) $dTA_0/dT_0 = -DbW/(1 + D)^2 < 0,$

(ii) $dTA_0/dt_0 = D(1 - b)W/(1 + D)^2 > 0,$

(iii) $dTA_0/dT = 0,$

(iv) $dTA_0/dt = 0.$

Clearly, permanent import tariffs and export taxes are equivalent policies as far as their trade balance effects are concerned, but temporary import tariffs and export taxes have opposite effects on the trade balance. Lerner symmetry therefore holds for permanent policies but not for temporary ones in this model. The trade balance in this model is identically equal to national saving under the assumption that there is no historical debt commitment. A permanent tariff or export tax does not affect incentives to save, that is, does not affect the consumption rate of interest, and therefore has no effect on the trade balance. (In addition, there is no effect on welfare since we are considering a small change in the tax/tariff beginning from free trade.) On the other hand, a temporary export tax *lowers* the domestic price of the exportable good and, other things being equal, lowers the price index in period 0. It follows that the cost of current consumption falls relative to the cost of future consumption, that is, the consumption rate rate of interest, falls. This stimulates current consumption, thereby reducing saving and the trade balance. In contrast, a temporary tariff *raises* the relative price of current goods (the consumption interest rate) and leads consumers to defer consumption and save more. Thus, the trade balance improves. The Lerner symmetry theorem was developed in the context of international trade models that ignored intertemporal considerations. Accordingly, in a model that takes account of such issues, one would expect that the theorem would be more likely to hold in the case of permanent policies than in the case of temporary ones.

Exercise III.5.3

Consider the model of chapter 5 where the representative agent consumes and receives endowments of importables and exportables in each period. There is no investment. Letting C_i denote the subutility index in period i, assume that agents maximize

$$U = [C_1^{1-1/\sigma} + DC_2^{1-1/\sigma}]/(1 - 1/\sigma), \tag{1}$$

where

$$C_i = [c_{xi}^{1-1/\varepsilon} + c_{mi}^{1-1/\varepsilon}]/(1 - 1/\varepsilon), \qquad t = 0, 1, \tag{2}$$

and where D is the subjective discount factor assumed to be equal to the world discount factor, and c_{xi} and c_{mi} denote, respectively, consumption of exportables and importables in period i, $i = 0, 1$. The parameter σ denotes the intertemporal elasticity of substitution while the parameter ε denotes the intratemporal elasticity of substitution between exportables and importables.

In this economy, the government levies a constant ad valorem tariff on imports in amount T in each period. The government redistributes the revenues from tariff collections to consumers in a lump-sum fashion. There is no government consumption.

a. Solve for the demands for C_i (the real spending functions) as a function of wealth, the discount factor, and the within-period consumer price indices.

b. Solve for the demands c_{xi} and c_{mi} as functions of within-period spending $P_i C_i$ and the within-period relative price. In this regard, you may assume that the world relative price is constant and equal to unity. You need not solve explicitly for P_i, but you should recall from the chapter that its elasticity with respect to the within-period relative price is equal to the expenditure share.

c. Consider the effect on the period 0 trade balance (measured in constant world prices) of an increase in the tariff in period 0 (with no change in the tariff in period 1). You may assume that the initial equilibrium is stationary in the sense that the expenditure share on importables (denoted by $1 - b$) and the price index P_i are constant through time. (Recall that the tariff rate, T, and world prices are constant in the initial equilibrium.) Does the temporary tariff cause the trade balance to "improve" or "deteriorate"? On what parameters of the utility function does your answer depend? Compare your answer to the one you got in the previous exercise, in which the parameters σ and ε were both assumed to be equal to unity.

Solution

a. To solve for the real spending functions, we maximize (1) subject to the constraint

$$P_0 C_0 + D P_1 C_1 = W, \tag{3}$$

where P_i is the consumer price index in period i and W is lifetime wealth (in terms of the numeraire, the exportable). Solving for the demand functions yields

$$C_0 = W/[P_0^\sigma(P_0^{1-\sigma} + DP_1^{1-\sigma})], \tag{4a}$$

$$C_1 = W/[P_1^\sigma(P_0^{1-\sigma} + DP_1^{1-\sigma})], \tag{4b}$$

where W (lifetime wealth) is given by

$$W = Y_{x0} + (1 + T_0)Y_{m0} + DY_{x1} + D(1 + T_1)Y_{m1} + G_0 + DG_1, \tag{5}$$

where G_i denotes government transfers (rebated tariff revenues) in period i which the consumer takes as given, and where for convenience we have assumed that world prices are constant and equal to unity.

b. To solve for the within-period demands for importables and exportables, we maximize (2) subject to the constraint

$$c_{xi} + (1 + T_i)c_{mi} = P_iC_i, \tag{6}$$

for $i = 0, 1$. Solving the first order conditions in the usual way gives

$$c_{xi} = P_iC_i/[1 + (1 + T_i)^{1-\varepsilon}], \tag{7a}$$

$$c_{mi} = P_iC_i/\{[1 + (1 + T_i)^{1-\varepsilon}](1 + T_i)^\varepsilon\}. \tag{7b}$$

c. The period 0 trade balance, measured in constant world prices, is

$$TA_0 = Y_{x0} + Y_{m0} - c_{x0} - c_{m0}. \tag{8}$$

To solve for the effect of a change in t_0 on the trade balance, we need to totally differentiate equation (8) taking into account the expressions for the demand functions c_{x0} and c_{m0} given in (7a) and (7b), which in turn depend on the real spending function C_0 given in (4a), the definition of lifetime wealth given in (5), and the budget constraints of the government, which imply

$$G_0 = T_0(c_{m0} - Y_{m0}), \tag{9a}$$

$$G_1 = T_1(c_{m1} - Y_{m1}). \tag{9b}$$

Clearly, since wealth depends on the present value of current and future transfers from the government, and future transfers depend on future imports, account must also be taken of equation (7b) for $i = 1$, and therefore of (4b) on which it depends. Proceeding in this way gives

$$dTA_0/dT_0 = \{DW(1 - b)/[(1 + T)^2(1 + D)^2]\}[(1 + Tb)\sigma - Tb\varepsilon], \tag{10}$$

where we have used the assumptions of an initially constant price index and expenditure share on importables, $1 - b$. Notice that if the initial tariff rate T is equal to zero, and the intertemporal and intratemporal elasticities of substitution (σ and ε) are equal to unity, then the expression in (10) is identical to the expression in equation ii in exercise III.5.2 (recalling that T denotes the tariff here rather than t).

It is clear from equation (10) that raising an initially positive tariff may have qualitatively different effects on the trade balance from those associated with the imposition of a small tariff from an initial position of free trade. In the latter case, we saw in the previous exercise that the intertemporal substitution effect ensured that a temporary tariff caused agents to save more, thereby improving the trade balance. This effect is still present in the case (see the first term on the RHS of equation 10), but there is also a distortion-magnification effect (second term) which operates in the opposite direction. Raising the tariff in period 0 magnifies a consumption distortion in that period by discouraging consumption of importables that are already underconsumed owing to the preexisting tariff and thereby causes real income to decline. Since the decline in real income is temporary (recall that the tariff in period 1 is not being altered), the permanent-income theory implies that agents will adjust their consumption somewhat less than the transitory decline in real income, thereby dissaving in period 0. The magnitude of the real income decline depends on ε since this parameter determines to what extent agents substitute between importables and exportables, and hence to what extent the initial distortion is magnified (see the second term in equation 10). Clearly, therefore, if σ is sufficiently small, a temporary tariff might actually cause the trade balance to deteriorate in the case in which there is an initial distortion, even though it necessarily generates an improvement in the trade balance from an initial position of free trade.

Exercise III.5.4

This exercise focuses on the effects of macroeconomic uncertainty on the current account. We consider a simple two-period economy with a tradable consumption good c and a tradable production good z. The relative price between c and z is fixed on world markets and for convenience set equal to unity. There is perfect capital mobility so the country can borrow and lend at a fixed world interest rate subject only to its intertemporal solvency constraint. The world interest rate is the yield on a real bond, which is the only asset in the model. In particular, complete markets that would allow the country to trade contingent claims for every state of nature are not assumed to exist. Thus, shocks to national output z are assumed to be nondiversifiable.

The representative agent is assumed to maximize the following intertemporal utility function:

$$u(c_1) + \frac{1}{(1 + r)} E\{u(c_2)\}, \tag{1}$$

where we assume that $u'(\cdot) > 0$, $u''(\cdot) < 0$, $u'''(\cdot) > 0$. To simplify matters, we have set the rate of time preference in equation (1) equal to the fixed world interest rate. The restrictions on the derivatives of the utility function reflect our assumption that *marginal* utility is convex. This assumption would be satisfied, for instance, if behavior exhibited decreasing absolute risk aversion, which seems plausible.

The maximization is subject to the intertemporal budget constraint

$$c_1 + \frac{c_2}{(1 + r)} = z_1 + \frac{z_2}{(1 + r)}, \tag{2}$$

where z is output and can be taken to be exogenous. The budget constraint embodies the assumption of perfect capital mobility, since the country is assumed to be able to borrow or lend at the exogenous interest rate, r. Because the constraint (2) is required to hold for all states of nature, it also reflects our assumption that complete markets for state-contingent claims do not exist.

a. Write down the first-order condition for an optimum.

b. If there is no uncertainty concerning output in period 2, show that consumption is equated across periods. If national output is constant over time, show that the country runs a zero current account balance (assume zero initial assets).

c. Suppose now that output is uncertain in period 2 but that the *expected* value of future output and current output are equal. What happens to consumption in this case? Does the country continue to run a zero current account balance?

Solution

a. The first-order condition for an optimum is

$$u_c(c_1) = E\{u_c(c_2)\}. \tag{3}$$

The fact that current marginal utility is equated to expected future marginal utility reflects the assumption (in equation 1) that the rate of time preference is equal to the world interest rate. This implies that there is no incentive to *tilt* the consumption profile as a result of divergences between subjective and world discount rates.

b. If there is no uncertainty about the evolution of output, then we have immediately from (3) that

$$u_c(c_1) = u_c(c_2). \tag{4}$$

Given that utility is convex, we have immediately from (4) that consumption is equated across the two periods, i.e., $c_1 = c_2$.

If output is constant over time ($z_1 = z_2 = \bar{z}$), then we also have from the intertemporal budget constraint (equation 2) that

$$c_1 = c_2 = z_1 = z_2 = \bar{z} \tag{5}$$

and therefore that the current account is in balance:

$$ca_1 = z_1 - c_1 = 0. \tag{6}$$

This result is scarcely surprising, and follows from the intertemporal symmetry that has been assumed.

c. Now suppose that, instead of the certain output in period 2, $\bar{z}$, the consumer faces some general form of ex ante uncertainty about future output, z_2; specifically, assume that

$$z_2 = \bar{z} + \zeta, \tag{7}$$

where ζ has mean zero, and variance σ_ζ^2. Defining marginal utility $v(\cdot) = u_c(\cdot)$, it follows from the first-order condition, and from Jensen's inequality,[2] that

$$c_1 = v^{-1}(E\{v(c_2)\}) < E\{c_2\}. \tag{8}$$

Since $c_1 < E\{c_2\}$, and $E\{z_2\} = z_1$, it follows from the intertemporal budget constraint that $c_1 < z_1$ and, therefore, that the country runs a current account surplus in period 1. Thus the presence of risk itself (and convex marginal utility) suffices to induce a surplus on the current account. Essentially, the existence of uncertainty, and hence the need to insure oneself against possible adverse shocks to output in the future, creates a *precautionary* demand for savings in period 1 that causes agents to reduce their consumption in that period. This precautionary demand for savings is reflected in the current account.

References for Part III: [5], [6], [7], [11], [23], [24], [34], [42].

---

2. Jensen's inequality states that, for any convex function $g(x)$, $E[g(x)] \geq g(E[x])$.

IV

An Intertemporal Approach to Fiscal Policies in the World Economy

6   Government Spending

Exercise IV.6.1

Consider a two-country model of the world economy. In each period t, the home country is completely specialized in the production of good X_t and, similarly, the foreign country is completely specialized in the production of good M_t, $t = 1, 2$. Let p_t denote the relative price of good X_t, that is, the terms of trade of the home country, and let M_t serve as numeraire throughout. Let R denote the world discount factor in terms of the foreign good. The budget constraint of the representative consumer living in the home country is

$$p_1 c_{x1} + c_{m1} + R(p_2 c_{x2} + c_{m2})$$
$$= p_1(X_1 - I_1 - T_1) + Rp_2[X_2(K_1 + I_1) - T_2], \tag{1}$$

where I_1 represents the level of domestic investment; c_{xt} and c_{mt} denote consumption of home and foreign goods in period t; K_1 is the initial capital stock; and the technology $X_2(\cdot)$ satisfies $X_2' > 0$ and $X_2'' < 0$. Tax liabilities in period t are denoted T_t. A corresponding constraint holds for the representative consumer living in the foreign country,

$$p_1 c_{x1}^* + c_{m1}^* + R(p_2 c_{x2}^* + c_{m2}^*)$$
$$= (M_1 - I_1^* - T_1^*) + R[M_2^*(K_1^* + I_1^*) - T_2^*], \tag{2}$$

where an asterisk denotes a corresponding foreign variable and where the technology $M_2(\cdot)$ satisfies $M_2' > 0$ and $M_2'' < 0$.

a. Show that I_1 is an increasing function of the domestic discount factor Rp_2/p_1 while I_1^* is an increasing function of the foreign discount factor R.

b. Suppose that the representative consumer in the home country has the following utility function

$$U = [C_1^{1-1/\sigma} + DC_2^{1-1/\sigma}]/(1 - 1/\sigma), \tag{3}$$

where $C_t = c_{xt}^b c_{mt}^{1-b}$ and D is the subjective discount factor. The utility function in the foreign country is also CES and the period-utility function is also Cobb-Douglas. Assume further that preferences are identical so that $D = D^*$, $\sigma = \sigma^*$, and $b = b^*$ (where b^* denotes the expenditure share on good x). Consider an initial equilibrium in which government spending levels in both countries are optimally set; that is, government spending is zero in both countries. What is the effect of a temporary current-period increase in government spending undertaken by the home country on domestic and foreign investment levels? Consider both the case where the government spends on domestic goods and where it spends on foreign goods.

Solution

a. The level of I_1 solves

$$\underset{I_1}{\text{Max}} \ [Rp_2 X_2(K_1 + I_1) - p_1 I_1].$$

The first-order condition for this problem is

$$Rp_2 X_2' - p_1 = 0,$$

which may be rewritten as

$$1 = \tau R X_2'(K_1 + I_1),$$

where τ is the intertemporal terms-of-trade ratio p_2/p_1. Totally differentiating the first-order condition gives

$$dI/d \log(\tau R) = -X_2'/X_2'' \equiv \varepsilon > 0.$$

Similarly, producers in the foreign country solve

$$\underset{I_1^*}{\text{Max}} \ [RM_2(K_1^* + I_1^*) - I_1^*],$$

the first-order condition for which is

$$1 = RM_2',$$

which can be differentiated to yield

$$dI^*/d \log R = -M_2'/M_2'' = \varepsilon^* > 0.$$

b. We first solve for the real spending functions by maximizing (3) subject to the constraint

$$P_1 C_1 + RP_2 C_2 = W, \tag{4}$$

where as usual P_t is the exact price index in period t and W is wealth. Solving the first-order conditions yields demands of the form

$$C_1 = W/\{P_1[1 + (RP_2/P_1)^{1-\sigma}D^\sigma]\}, \tag{5a}$$

$$C_2 = W(RP_2/P_1)^{1-\sigma}D^\sigma/\{RP_2[1 + (RP_2/P_1)^{1-\sigma}D^\sigma]\}, \tag{5b}$$

and since under Cobb-Douglas utility we know that expenditure shares are constant, we have that

$$c_{x1} = bW/\{p_1[1 + (RP_2/P_1)^{1-\sigma}D^\sigma]\}, \tag{6a}$$

$$c_{m1} = (1 - b)W/\{[1 + (RP_2/P_1)^{1-\sigma}D^\sigma]\}, \tag{6b}$$

$$c_{x2} = bW(RP_2/P_1)^{1-\sigma}D^\sigma/\{Rp_2[1 + (RP_2/P_1)^{1-\sigma}D^\sigma]\}, \tag{6c}$$

$$c_{m2} = (1 - b)W(RP_2/P_1)^{1-\sigma}D^\sigma/\{R[1 + (RP_2/P_1)^{1-\sigma}D^\sigma]\}, \tag{6d}$$

where the price index $P_t = kp_t^b$ with $k = b^{-b}(1 - b)^{-b}$.[1] The demand functions of agents in the foreign country are derived in a similar fashion.

Four equilibrium conditions must be satisfied in this model, but by Walras's law we can ignore any one of them. Accordingly, we focus on the market-clearing conditions for good X in periods 1 and 2 and good M in period 1, which are given by

$$b(W + W^*)/\{p_1[1 + (RP_2/P_1)^{1-\sigma}D^\sigma]\} + I_1 + G_{x1} = X_1, \tag{7}$$

$$b(W + W^*)(RP_2/P_1)^{1-\sigma}D^\sigma/\{Rp_2[1 + (RP_2/P_1)^{1-\sigma}D^\sigma]\} = X_2, \tag{8}$$

$$(1 - b)(W + W^*)/\{[1 + (RP_2/P_1)^{1-\sigma}D^\sigma]\} + I_1^* + G_{m1} = M_1, \tag{9}$$

where we have imposed that foreign-government spending is zero in both periods and domestic-government spending is zero in period 2. To determine the effects of fiscal-policy shocks on domestic and foreign investment levels, we need to determine how investment rates of interest move in each country, and therefore how the intertemporal terms of trade ratio, τ, and the world discount factor, R, respond to changes in government spending. To do this, it is convenient to transform the three-equation system in p_1,

---

1. The formula for the price index can be derived by solving the cost-minimization problem of allocating within-period spending to consumption of the two goods. The Lagrange multiplier of that problem is the price index.

p_2, and R given by equations (7)–(9) into a two-equation system in τ and R by using the budget constraints of the government and the private sectors. Accordingly, from the righthand side of equation (1) and the requirement that the domestic government be intertemporally solvent, we have that

$$W = p_1(X_1 - I_1 - G_{x1} + R\tau X_2) - G_{m1} \tag{10}$$

and, similarly, using equation (2) we have that

$$W^* = M_1 - I_1^* + RM_2, \tag{11}$$

where we have assumed that there is no government spending in the foreign country. Adding together (7) and (8) and substituting for W by using (10) gives the condition

$$(1 - b)W + G_{m1} = bW^*, \tag{12}$$

which simply states that the present value of home-country imports equals the present value of foreign-country imports. Using (10) and (11) allows us now to solve for the terms of trade in period 1 as a function of R and τ, only

$$p_1 = b(M_1 - I_1^* - G_{m1} + RM_2)/[(1 - b)(X_1 - I_1 - G_{x1} + R\tau X_2)], \tag{13}$$

and substituting (13) back into (7) and (9) gives the following system in R and τ

$$X_1 - I_1 - G_{x1} = (X_1 - I_1 - G_{x1} + R\tau X_2)/[1 + (RP_2/P_1)^{1-\sigma}D^\sigma], \tag{14}$$

$$M_1 - I_1^* - G_{m1} = (M_1 - I_1^* - G_{m1} + RM_2)/[1 + (RP_2/P_1)^{1-\sigma}D^\sigma], \tag{15}$$

which can be totally differentiated to yield the effects of various fiscal-policy shocks on investment rates of interest at home and abroad. Consider first the case where the government increases its current spending on domestic goods. In this case, we have

$$d\log \tau/dG_{x1} = -(1 - b)(\sigma + s^*)/[b\Delta(M_1 - I_1^*)], \tag{16a}$$

$$d\log R/dG_{x1} = -(1 - b)(1 - \sigma)/[\Delta(M_1 - I_1^*)], \tag{16b}$$

$$d\log(R\tau)/dG_{x1} = -(1 - b)[b(1 - \sigma) + \sigma + s^*]/[b\Delta(M_1 - I_1^*)], \tag{16c}$$

where $\Delta = ss^* + s[1 - (1 - \sigma)(1 - b)] + s^*[1 - b(1 - \sigma)] + \sigma > 0$,

$s = \varepsilon[1 + D^{-\sigma}(RP_2/P_1)^{\sigma-1}]/(X_1 - I_1 - G_{x1}) > 0$,

$s^* = \varepsilon^*[1 + D^{-\sigma}(RP_2/P_1)^{\sigma-1}]/(M_1 - I_1^*) > 0$.

A temporary increase in government spending on the domestic good generates an improvement in the terms of trade for the home country in the first period relative to the second period; that is, causes τ to fall. The fall in τ raises the consumption rate of interest by making the domestic good, and hence the consumption basket, more expensive in period 1 relative to period 2, and this depresses current relative to future consumption. If consumptions in the two periods are very good substitutes, that is, if the intertemporal elasticity of substitution is sufficiently large (greater than unity in this case), the world interest rate in terms of importables may actually fall in response to the temporary fiscal expansion, since the change in the terms-of-trade ratio is more than sufficient to eliminate the excess demand for current goods at the initial interest rate. This is captured by equation (16b), which shows that the discount factor rises (the interest rate falls) if $\sigma > 1$ but falls (the interest rate rises) if $\sigma < 1$.

Adding (16a) and (16b) together shows that while the behavior of the world discount factor R depends on the value of the intertemporal elasticity of substitution, the behavior of the domestic discount factor $R\tau$ does not; that is, $R\tau$ always falls in response to a temporary increase in government spending on domestic goods. This means of course that with producer interest rates always rising in the home country, domestic investment is always crowded out by a temporary fiscal expansion that falls predominantly on domestic goods. By contrast, we have seen that the behavior of R depends on the value of the intertemporal elasticity of substitution σ. When $\sigma < 1$, R falls, and both domestic and foreign investments are crowded out. When, however, $\sigma > 1$, R will actually rise in response to the increase in government spending and this will cause producer interest rates to decline in the foreign country. Clearly, therefore, investment will actually increase in the foreign country in this case, even though domestic investment is crowded out. In this case, notwithstanding the assumption of full capital mobility, investment moves asymmetrically across the two countries in response to a temporary fiscal expansion. This is because investment decisions depend not only on the common world interest rate (the rate of return on the internationally traded bond in this model) but also on the time path of the terms of trade, which affects real rates of return on physical investments differently in the two countries.

Consider finally the case where the government spends on foreign goods. Differentiating equations (14) and (15) gives

$$d\log \tau/dG_{m1} = (\sigma + s)/[\Delta(M_1 - I_1^*)], \tag{17a}$$

$$d\log R/dG_{m1} = -[(1 - b)(1 - \sigma) + \sigma + s]/[\Delta(M_1 - I_1^*)], \tag{17b}$$

$$d \log(R\tau)/dG_{m1} = -(1 - b)[b(1 - \sigma)]/[b\Delta(M_1 - I_1^*)]. \tag{17c}$$

When the government increases spending on foreign goods, its terms of trade deteriorate temporarily and therefore τ rises. This reduces the price of current consumption relative to future consumption and ensures that, in order to eliminate the incipient excess demand for current goods created by the increase in government spending, the world discount factor must fall. It follows therefore that foreign investment must necessarily be crowded out by the fiscal expansion originating in the home country. This is not, however, true of domestic investment. Since the terms of trade improve in the future relative to the current period in this case (τ rises), this raises the profitability of domestic investments. Although the rise in the world discount factor R reduces the profitability of such investments, the behavior of the latter is influenced by the product $R\tau$ which may rise or fall depending on the value of the intertemporal elasticity of substitution. If this elasticity is greater than unity, equation (17c) shows that the domestic discount factor rises in response to the fiscal expansion, and investment rates of interest fall. In this case, therefore, investment rises in the domestic economy. We conclude that, when fiscal-policy shocks induce sharp movements in the terms of trade, investment expenditures need not move together in different countries even in the presence of full capital mobility. A key parameter influencing the behavior of investment is the intertemporal elasticity of substitution in consumption.

Exercise IV.6.2

Consider the two-country model developed in the previous exercise. Can a temporary fiscal expansion lead to a negative comovement between consumption growth rates at home and abroad? Discuss.

Solution

Dividing equation (5b) by equation (5a) of the previous exercise allows one to solve for (1 plus) the growth rate of consumption as

$$1 + g = (RP_2/P_1)^{-\sigma}D^\sigma, \tag{1}$$

where g denotes the growth rate of aggregate consumption. Clearly, because preferences are homothetic, the consumption growth rate is independent of the wealth level and depends only on the intertemporal relative price, that is, the consumption discount factor RP_2/P_1. From the definition of the consumer price index, we can rewrite (1) as

$$1 + g = (R\tau^b)^{-\sigma} D^\sigma, \tag{1'}$$

where τ is the intertemporal terms-of-trade ratio p_2/p_1 and b is the expenditure share on exportables. Equation (1') shows clearly that the behavior of the consumption growth rate in response to fiscal-policy shocks depends only on the behaviors of R and τ, which are of course common to both countries. With identical preferences, D, b, and σ are also the same in both countries so that consumption growth rates will always change by exactly the same amount independent of the nature of the fiscal-policy shock being considered. This is a reflection both of the assumption of identical preferences and of free trade in goods and financial assets. For convenience, the change in the consumption growth rate (in both countries) is given by

$$d\log(1 + g) = -\sigma[d\log R + bd\log \tau], \tag{2}$$

which, by using (16a)–(16b) and (17a)–(17b) of the previous exercise, may be written as

$$d\log(1 + g)/dG_{x1} = \sigma(1 - b)(1 + s^*)/[\Delta(M_1 - I_1^*)], \tag{3}$$

$$d\log(1 + g)/dG_{m1} = \sigma(1 - b)(1 + s)/[\Delta(M_1 - I_1^*)]. \tag{4}$$

Clearly, therefore, a temporary increase in government spending raises the growth rate of consumption in both countries independent of the commodity composition of government expenditures. The reason is that a temporary increase in government consumption creates an incipient excess demand for current-relative-to-future goods which requires that private consumption be crowded out. The mechanism through which this is achieved is an increase in consumption rates of interest in both countries (a decrease in the consumption discount factor) which causes consumers to postpone their expenditures. Because the consumption rate of interest depends only on the behavior of world prices (there being no nontraded goods in the model) and because preferences are identical, consumption growth rates must move together in response to the fiscal expansion.

Exercise IV.6.3

Consider a two-country model of the world economy. In each period t, each country receives endowments of two goods, X_t and M_t for the home country and X_t^* and M_t^* for the foreign country, where the first good is assumed to be exported by the home country, the second is imported by the home country, and $t = 1, 2$. The world relative price of importables is denoted p_t and the world discount factor is R. The numeraire is the home country's exportable. There is no investment. The budget constraint of the representative consumer living in the home country is

$$c_{x1} + p_1(1 + \tau_1)c_{m1} + R[c_{x2} + p_2(1 + \tau_2)c_{m2}]$$
$$= [X_1 + p_1(1 + \tau_1)M_1 + G_1] + R[X_2 + p_2(1 + \tau_2)M_2 + G_2]$$
$$\equiv W, \tag{1}$$

where τ_t is an ad valorem tariff levied by the government of the home country on imports $(c_{mt} - M_t)$ and G_t denotes government spending on transfers which consumers take as given. The government's budget constraint satisfies

$$G_1 + DG_2 = \tau_1 p_1 c_{m1} + R\tau_2 p_2 c_{m2}. \tag{2}$$

In the foreign country, the consumer's budget constraint is given by

$$c_{x1}^* + p_1 c_{m1}^* + R(c_{x2}^* + p_2 c_{m2}^*) = (X_1^* + p_1 M_1^*) + R(X_2^* + p_2 M_2^*) \equiv W^*, \tag{3}$$

where it has been assumed that there is no tariff in the foreign country, and where an asterisk denotes a corresponding foreign-economy variable. Suppose preferences in the home country are given by

$$U = \log[c_{x1}^b c_{m1}^{1-b}] + D\log[c_{x2}^b c_{m2}^{1-b}], \tag{4}$$

where $0 < b < 1$ and D is the subjective discount factor. Assume that preferences in the foreign country are of the same form and that $b = b^*$ and $D = D^*$.

a. Beginning from an initial equilibrium of free trade (that is, $\tau_1 = \tau_2 = 0$), find the effect on relative prices p_1 and p_2 of the imposition of a permanent tariff; that is, $d\tau_1 = d\tau_2 = d\tau > 0$.

b. Find the effect on the period 1 trade balance of the permanent tariff. You may assume that initially the trade account balance is equal to zero. How does your answer compare to the answer you got in exercise III.5.2 for the case of a small country? Discuss.

Solution

a. Given that the budget constraints (1) and (3) are satisfied, goods-market equilibrium can be summarized by the conditions

$$c_{m1} + c^*_{m1} = M_1 + M^*_1, \tag{5}$$

$$c_{m2} + c^*_{m2} = M_2 + M^*_2, \tag{6}$$

$$c_{x1} + c^*_{x1} = X_1 + X^*_1, \tag{7}$$

where we have omitted the equilibrium condition corresponding to second-period home-country exportables, and where the demand functions are given by

$$c_{x1} = bW/(1 + D), \tag{8a}$$

$$c_{m1} = (1 - b)W/[(1 + \tau_1)p_1(1 + D)], \tag{8b}$$

$$c_{x2} = DbW/[R(1 + D)], \tag{8c}$$

$$c_{m2} = D(1 - b)W/[R(1 + \tau_2)p_2(1 + D)], \tag{8d}$$

and analogously for the foreign country. Totally differentiating equations (5)–(7) allows us to solve for the effects on p_1, p_2, and R of a permanent tariff of size $d\tau$. Assuming that the initial equilibrium is one of free trade, we have

$$d\log p_1/d\tau = -s, \tag{9a}$$

$$d\log p_2/d\tau = -s, \tag{9b}$$

$$d\log R/d\tau = 0, \tag{9c}$$

where $0 < s = W/(W + W^*) < 1$ denotes the share of domestic wealth in world wealth.

b. The home country's trade balance measured in real terms evaluated at world prices is

$$TA = [(X_1 - c_{x1}) - p_1(c_{m1} - M_1)]/P_1(p_1). \tag{10}$$

Clearly, under the assumption that $TA = 0$ in the initial equilibrium, it makes no difference whether we consider the effect of changing the tariff on the real trade balance TA or the "nominal" trade balance $P_1 TA$. Totally differentiating equation (10) around an initial equilibrium with $TA = 0$ gives

$$dTA/d\tau = s\gamma(1 - b)(\mu_{m2} - \mu_{m1})C_1, \tag{11}$$

where $0 < \gamma = RP_2 C_2/W < 1$ denotes the average saving propensity and $0 < \mu_{mt} = M_t/c_{mt} < 1$ denotes the ratio of the endowment to the consumption of the importable good.

The intuition of the expression in equation (11) is as follows: The imposition of a tariff in periods 1 and 2 improves the terms of trade of the tariff-imposing country (equations 9a and 9b) but leaves the world interest rate unchanged. This is the familiar result from static trade theory that, because the country has some "monopoly" power in trade, restricting its demand for imports causes the world relative price of home country imports to fall, an improvement in the home country's terms of trade. The magnitude of the improvement in the terms of trade is governed by the size of the country imposing the tariff, as measured by the parameter s which equals the home country's share of world wealth (which also equals its share of world consumption of either of the two goods). In the small-country case analyzed in exercise III.5.2, s tends to zero so that there is no improvement in the terms of trade. Since s multiplies the entire expression in equation (11), it is clear that in the small-country case the tariff has no effect on the trade balance either, which was the result obtained in that exercise.[2]

In the large-country case, the improvement in the terms of trade raises real income by an amount that depends on the parameter μ_{mt}. If $\mu_{m2} > \mu_{m1}$, then the increase in real income is greater in period 1 than in period 2 because the economy is closer to the autarky equilibrium in period 2 than in period 1; recall that in the autarky case $\mu_{mt} = 1$ and the real income gain associated with the improvement in the terms of trade is minimized and equal to zero. With current real income above its long-run level, consumers will smooth their consumption stream relative to their income stream by increasing their savings, and the trade balance will improve. Conversely, when the real income gain is expected to be relatively large in the future; that is, when $\mu_{m2} < \mu_{m1}$, the trade balance deteriorates as consumers find it optimal to borrow against part of their future income gain. In the special case in which the income gains associated with the terms-of-trade improvement are equal in both periods, so that $\mu_{m2} = \mu_{m1}$, there is no change in the trade balance since current income and permanent income are equal and agents have no incentive to borrow or lend in international capital markets.

---

2. Recall that this result was obtained in the case of a permanent tariff only; temporary tariffs were shown to have effects on the trade balance even in the absence of terms-of-trade effects, that is, when the tariff-imposing country is small.

7

Budget Deficits with Nondistortionary Taxes: The Pure Wealth Effect

Exercise IV.7.1

Consider an endowment economy where dynasties, in contrast to the model in chapter 7, have infinite lives. Suppose that new cohorts enter the economy in each period (for example, because of immigration) and that the total population grows at a constant rate, n. While new entrants have no initial debt they are otherwise identical to existing dynasties. In particular, all agents have identical endowments (labor incomes) and are subject to the same lump-sum taxes. Suppose that preferences of an agent born at time s can be described by a logarithmic utility function,

$$U(s) = \sum_{s}^{\infty} \delta^t \ln\{c(s, t)\}, \tag{1}$$

where δ denotes the subjective discount factor $(0 < \delta < 1)$ and $c(s, t)$ is consumption in period t of an agent born at time s $(s \leq t)$.
a. Describe the optimal consumption path and debt allocation for agents born in period s.
b. Find the *aggregate* consumption path and the law of motion for the different types of wealth. Explain why the relevant private-sector discount rates are different for human capital and financial assets/debt.
c. Show that, for $n > 0$, Ricardian neutrality does not hold even though agents have infinite horizons.

Solution

a. Consumers maximize their expected utility as described in equation (1) subject to an infinite horizon budget constraint. In any period t, the budget constraint for a consumer born at time s is

$$\sum_{j=0}^{\infty} \alpha_j c(s, t + j) = R(t - 1)b^p(t - 1) + \sum_{j=0}^{\infty} \alpha_j y(t + j)$$

$$\equiv w^p(s, t) \qquad \text{for all } s \le t, \tag{2}$$

where the discount factor is defined as $\alpha_j = 1/(R_t R_{t+1} \ldots R_{t+j-1})$, $\alpha_0 \equiv 1$, $R(t + j)$ denotes the interest factor in period $t + j$, and $w^p(s, t)$ is private wealth in period t of a consumer born at time s. According to equation (2) the present value of private consumption cannot exceed the present value of disposable income (y) and the initial value of private-sector financial wealth $(R(t - 1)b^p(t - 1))$. Equation (2) implicitly assumes that the private-sector solvency condition applies; that is, private Ponzi schemes are ruled out.

Solving the consumer's problem yields the standard first-order conditions for optimal consumption choice equalizing marginal utility of consumption and the relevant marginal costs

$$\delta^j \frac{1}{c(s, t + j)} = \lambda \alpha_j \qquad \text{for all } j, s \le t. \tag{3}$$

The parameter λ denotes the Lagrange multiplier associated with the budget constraint in equation (2). Using equation (3) and the definition of private wealth in equation (2), optimal consumption turns out to be a constant fraction of the consumer's wealth

$$c(s, t) = (1 - \delta)w^p(s, t)$$

$$\equiv (1 - \delta)[R(t - 1)b^p(s, t - 1) + h(t)] \qquad \text{for all } t \ge s. \tag{4}$$

It will be convenient to divide consumer wealth into financial wealth $(R(t - 1)b^p(s, t - 1))$ and human wealth $h(t)$, the latter meaning the present value of disposable income. Note that by assumption newcomers and existing cohorts have the same disposable-income stream so that $h(s, t) = h(t)$ for all $s \le t$. The proportionality of consumption and wealth, with the factor of proportionality $(1 - \delta)$ independent of the interest rate, is a standard feature for logarithmic utility functions. As a result, the accumulation of financial assets and debt holdings is determined by the time profile of the consumer's income stream.

b. To find the aggregate consumption path and the laws of motion for financial and human wealth, we can use the assumption that the relevant population size is increasing at a constant rate, n. Per capita aggregates are weighted sums across all cohorts, with the weights depending on a cohort's relative population size. To facilitate the exposition, we shall write explicitly the one-period budget constraints at time t for different cohorts

$$c(0, t) + b^p(0, t) = R(t - 1)b^p(0, t - 1) + y(t) \quad \text{for cohort born at } t = 0$$

$$c(s, t) + b^p(s, t) = R(t - 1)b^p(s, t - 1) + y(t) \quad \text{for cohort born at } s < t$$

$$c(t, t) + b^p(t, t) = R(t - 1)b^p(t, t - 1) + y(t) \quad \text{for cohort born at } t$$

$$= y(t). \tag{5}$$

The last part of equation (5) reflects that cohorts who join the population have initially no financial assets or debts: $b^p(t, t - 1) = 0$. Aggregating equation (5) across cohorts and dividing by the population size at time t gives the evolution of private per capita debt

$$B^p(t) = \frac{R(t - 1)}{1 + n} B^p(t - 1) + Y(t) - C(t). \tag{6}$$

In equation (6) and below, per capita aggregates are denoted by capital letters. The relevant discount factor for per capita private debt is the rate of return on financial assets, R, adjusted by the population growth factor, $1 + n$. The latter reflects that newcomers differ from existing populations because they are not endowed with financial assets. Ceteris paribus, average private-asset holdings in the economy would decline from period t to $t + 1$ since the population base for calculating the per capita asset value increases at rate n.

Consumption of all cohorts is proportional to their private wealth, or the sum of financial and human wealth (see equation 4). The same holds consequently for per capita consumption

$$C(t) = (1 - \delta)\left\{\frac{R(t - 1)}{1 + n} B^p(t - 1) + H(t)\right\}$$

$$= (1 - \delta)W^p(t). \tag{7}$$

In deriving equation (7), we used the fact that all cohorts receive the same future disposable-income streams so that aggregate per capita human wealth is identical to human wealth of any cohort alive: $H(t) = h(t)$. Note that the value of per capita financial assets in the consumption function is corrected for the rate of population growth. This correction, however, does not apply to the second component of private wealth (W^p), the per capita present value of the return on human capital (H). The distinction between the two forms of wealth becomes more evident when we derive the law of motion for human wealth and compare it to the previously derived law of motion for financial assets. With all individuals receiving the same future disposable-income streams, per capita human wealth at times t and $t - 1$ is

$H(t) = h(t)$

$$= y(t) + \frac{1}{R(t)} y(t + 1) + \frac{1}{R(t)R(t + 1)} y(t + 2) + \cdots \tag{8a}$$

$H(t - 1) = h(t - 1)$

$$= y(t - 1) + \frac{1}{R(t - 1)} y(t) + \frac{1}{R(t - 1)R(t)} y(t + 1) + \cdots. \tag{8b}$$

Combining the two parts of the equation gives the law of motion for human wealth

$$H(t) = R(t - 1)[H(t - 1) - Y(t - 1)]. \tag{9}$$

The relevant interest rate that links per capita human wealth across time is thus the market interest rate R. This contrasts with the financial-asset component of wealth, where the effective interest rate incorporates the population growth factor as described in equation (6).

Finally, to find the time path for total per capita wealth we can use the result already applied in the consumption function; that is, $W^P(t) = R(t - 1)/(1 + n) B^P(t - 1) + H(t)$. Inserting the previously derived laws of motion for per capita private assets and human wealth and rearranging terms yields the corresponding path for total wealth

$$W^P(t) = \frac{R(t - 1)}{1 + n} \delta W^P(t - 1) + \frac{n}{1 + n} H(t). \tag{10}$$

For the case of zero population growth, the standard result reemerges whereby wealth is proportional across time with the factor of proportionality depending on the rate of interest and the agent's time preference. In particular, if time preference and interest rate are equal, so that $R\delta = 1$, per capita wealth would remain constant over time. With nonzero population growth, the exclusive dependence of wealth on past wealth levels is broken. The law of motion depends instead in a separate way also on the level of human wealth in the current period, the last term in equation (10).

c. The objective of this section is to show within the previously developed framework that the timing of government taxes can have real effects. It is assumed that the government's lump-sum taxes are the same for members of all cohorts and that the government's solvency condition is satisfied. Under these assumptions, the government's intertemporal budget constraint at time t can be expressed in terms of per capita values as

$$\sum_{j=0}^{\infty} \alpha_j (1 + n)^j G(t + j) = \frac{R(t - 1)}{1 + n} B^g(t - 1) + \sum_{j=0}^{\infty} \alpha_j (1 + n)^j T(t + j), \tag{11}$$

where G and T denote per capita government spending and taxes, respectively. Similarly to the valuation of financial assets in the private-sector budget constraint, the per capita return on government assets (B^g) depends on population growth. For example, a per capita debt of $100 in period $t - 1$ would amount to a per capita debt of $100/(1 + n)$ at the beginning of period t since newly arriving agents initially carry no government assets.

Suppose the government institutes a tax cut in period 0. This is followed by a uniform tax increase in all future periods to maintain government solvency. Assuming that the interest rate remains constant and that the government spending path remains unchanged, we can derive the necessary tax adjustments in future periods by differentiating equation (11):[1]

$$dT(0) = -\frac{1}{\dfrac{R}{1+n} - 1} dT. \tag{12}$$

The implications of a tax cut for future tax liabilities depend on the population growth rate. A given tax cut in period 0 requires smaller future tax increases for larger values of n: If the number of new arrivals is higher, more future taxpayers will share the tax burden, thereby reducing the tax burden for each individual.

Changes in government tax policies affect private consumption if they alter the value of human wealth. Human wealth is a function of disposable income, that is, labor income (Y^l) net of taxes: $Y(t) = Y^l(t) - T(t)$. The effects of the temporary tax cut on human wealth can be determined by combining equation (12) with the definition of human wealth for period 0 (compare equation 8):

$$\frac{dH(0)}{dT(0)} = -\frac{R}{R - 1}\left\{1 - \frac{1}{1+n}\right\} \leq 0. \tag{13}$$

A tax cut in period 0 followed by compensating tax increases in future periods increases the present value of disposable-income streams if $n > 0$. The rationale for this result stems from the differences among groups affected by the tax cut in period 0 and those burdened with future tax liabilities. The effect of the tax cut is enjoyed only by consumers currently populating the economy. The future tax burden, on the other hand, is also shared by those who will enter the economy in future periods. The net effect of the tax cut for the current beneficiaries is thus a rise in the present value of their disposable income. The increase in wealth leads to an increase

---

1. The derivation of equation (12) is subject to an upper bound on n: $n < R - 1$.

in current-period per capita consumption. Combining equations (7) and (13), the effect is

$$\frac{dC(0)}{dT(0)} = -(1 - \delta)\frac{R}{R - 1}\left\{1 - \frac{1}{1 + n}\right\} \leq 0. \tag{14}$$

The result demonstrates that real allocations are generally not neutral with respect to the timing of lump-sum taxes. The breakdown in the Ricardian neutrality proposition arises here despite the infinite planning horizon of all agents. Instead, the arrival of new agents has implications similar to the finiteness of the planning horizon. Government deficits are not neutral since intertemporal shifts in taxes affect cohorts in the economy differently, depending on the cohort's arrival date. Beneficiaries of a current tax cut are only those currently present, while future taxes that finance the current tax cuts are also shared by later arrivals to the economy.

Exercise IV.7.2

Consider the infinite horizon, overlapping generations model with nonzero population growth that was developed in exercise IV.7.1. Suppose the government enacts a temporary tax cut followed by future tax increases that leave the government's spending path unchanged. Calculate the value of the current-consumption multiplier for alternative lengths of the tax-cut period and different values of the population growth rate. Assume that the interest-rate factor $R = 1.05$ and the subjective discount factor $\delta = .95$, and let the time interval for the tax cut range from one to seven periods. Compare the results to the effects of varying life expectancies in the model of chapter 7.

Solution

The effects of tax cuts of different lengths can be derived similarly to the derivation of a one-period tax cut (see equations 12–14 in exercise IV.7.1). For example, to maintain government solvency in the case of a tax cut that extends from period 0 to period 2, future taxes must rise according to

$$-\left\{\frac{R^2}{(1 + n)^2} + \frac{R}{1 + n} + 1\right\}\left\{\frac{R}{1 + n} - 1\right\}dT(0) = dT,$$

$$\text{for } dT(0) = dT(1) = dT(2). \tag{1}$$

Accordingly, per capita human wealth, or the present value of the disposable-income stream, increases after this tax cut by $dH(0)/dT(0) =$

$-R/(R-1)(1-[1/(1+n)]^3)$ and the increase in period 0 consumption is given by

$$\frac{dC(0)}{dT(0)} = -(1-\delta)\frac{R}{R-1}\left\{1 - \frac{1}{(1+n)^3}\right\}, \quad \text{for } dT(0) = dT(1) = dT(2).$$

(2)

Similarly, one can derive the effect on consumption for an arbitrary finite length $j \geq 1$ of the current tax cut. The effect on current-period consumption is

$$\frac{dC(0)}{dT(0)} = -(1-\delta)\frac{R}{R-1}\left\{1 - \frac{1}{(1+n)^j}\right\},$$

$$\text{for } dT(0) = dT(1) = \cdots = dT(j). \quad (3)$$

The effect of a tax cut on current-period consumption is stronger the longer the tax cut is in effect ($\partial[dC(0)/dT(0)]/\partial j < 0$ for $n > 0$). The result reflects the fact that all people currently alive will benefit from a tax cut in period j. On the other hand, they will share only part of the future tax burden since it will also fall on agents joining the economy in period $j + 1$ and thereafter.

Frenkel and Razin derive the analogue of equation (3) for the case of zero population growth ($n = 0$) when agents have a finite expected lifetime. For the case of logarithmic utility and constant period-survival probability ($\gamma \leq 1$), the corresponding equation is

$$\frac{dC(0)}{dT(0)} = -(1-\gamma\delta)\frac{R}{R-\gamma}(1-\gamma^j), \quad \text{for } dT(0) = dT(1)\cdots = dT(j). \quad (4)$$

Note that in their case Ricardian neutrality reemerges if agents have infinite horizons ($\gamma = 1$), while in the case that allows for population growth neutrality requires that their arrival rate is zero ($n = 0$). Only in these cases would temporary tax cuts have no effect on consumption.

The Ricardian neutrality result is reported in the first column of table 1. The table also reports the simulation results of equations (3) and (4) for alternative values of the arrival and survival parameters (n and γ) and for various lengths of the current-period tax cut. The values of the multipliers reported in the table are considerably lower for the model with population growth than for the model with finite horizons. Yet a comparison in this form is rather tenuous. Depending on which of the two models would describe the real world more accurately, the implications for other parame-

Table 1
Current consumption multiplier for alternative length of current tax-cut period

a. Model with infinite horizon and population growth ($\gamma = 1, n \geq 0$)

Length of current tax-cut period (t)	Population growth (n)						
	0	0.005	0.01	0.015	0.02	0.03	0.05
1	0	0.01	0.02	0.03	0.04	0.06	0.10
3	0	0.02	0.04	0.06	0.08	0.12	0.19
5	0	0.03	0.06	0.09	0.12	0.17	0.27
7	0	0.04	0.08	0.12	0.15	0.22	0.34

b. Model with finite horizon and no population growth ($\gamma \leq 1, n = 0$)

Length of current tax-cut period (t)	Survival probability (γ)			
	1	0.9	0.85	0.8
1	0	0.19	0.28	0.36
3	0	0.35	0.48	0.60
5	0	0.48	0.63	0.74
7	0	0.58	0.74	0.84

Note: The multipliers in panel a are based on equation (3) and those in panel b are based on equation (4). The length of the tax cut is 1 plus the length reported in the table ($j = t + 1$).

ters, in particular δ, are likely to be quite different. Moreover, both models may be complementary rather than mutually exclusive and the "true" multiplier, if it were different from zero, could reflect their combined effect (see also exercise IV.7.3).

Exercise IV.7.3

Consider the overlapping generations model of chapter 7 where agents have a constant survival probability (γ). In extension of the model, suppose that new cohorts arrive each period as described in exercise IV.7.1. Consequently, total population is growing at a constant rate, n. For simplicity, assume that an agent's preferences can be described by a logarithmic expected-utility function.

a. Derive the optimal consumption path and the laws of motion for different types of wealth.

b. Explain the conditions for debt neutrality. Show that the results in chapter 7 and exercise IV.7.1 emerge as special cases.

Solution

a. The exercise combines features of the finite-lifetime model in Frenkel and Razin with the population growth model developed in exercise IV.7.1. We begin by deriving the optimal consumption choice for individuals belonging to a cohort born at time s. Their preferences at the beginning of period t are described by the following logarithmic expected-utility function:

$$E\{U(s)\} = E\left\{\sum_{j=0}^{\infty} \delta^j \ln\{c(s, t+j)\}\right\} \quad \text{for } s \leq t \tag{1a}$$

where δ denotes the subjective discount factor $(0 < \delta < 1)$, E is the expectations operator, and $c(s, t)$ is consumption in period t of an agent born at time s $(s \leq t)$. With constant period-survival probability $(\gamma \leq 1)$ as the only source of uncertainty, the certainty equivalence form of the preference function in equation (1a) is

$$\sum_{j=0}^{\infty} (\gamma\delta)^j \ln\{c(s, t+j)\} \quad \text{for } s \leq t. \tag{1b}$$

The consumer's problem is to maximize the preference function as described in equation (1b) subject to a sequence of one-period budget constraints:

$$c(s, t) + b^P(s, t+1) = \frac{R(t-1)}{\gamma} b^P(s, t-1) + y(s, t). \tag{2}$$

Consolidating the one-period budget constraints and imposing the solvency condition yields the intertemporal budget constraint for an agent born at time $s \leq t$:

$$\sum_{j=0}^{\infty} \gamma^j \alpha_j c(s, t+j) = \frac{R(t-1)}{\gamma} b^P(s, t-1) + \sum_{j=0}^{\infty} \gamma^j \alpha_j y(s, t+j)$$

$$\equiv w^P(s, t), \tag{3}$$

where the discount factor is defined as $\alpha_j = 1/[R(t)R(t+1)\ldots R(t+j-1)]$, $\alpha_0 \equiv 1$, $R(t+j)$ denotes the interest factor in period $t+j$, and $w^P(s, t)$ is private wealth in period t of a consumer born at time s. Since the probability of death is nonzero, the effective discount rate is the interest rate adjusted by the probability of survival: $\gamma^j \alpha_j$.

Solving the consumer's problem yields the necessary conditions for optimal consumption choice:

$$(\gamma\delta)^j \frac{1}{c(s, t+j)} = \lambda\gamma^j\alpha_j \quad \text{for all } j, s \leq t. \tag{4}$$

In equilibrium, the marginal utility of consumption equals the relevant marginal cost of consumption. The latter includes the shadow value associated with the budget constraint (λ). Using equation (4) and the definition of private wealth in equation (3), equilibrium consumption is found to be a constant fraction of the consumer's wealth:

$$c(s, t) = (1 - \gamma\delta)w^P(s, t)$$

$$\equiv (1 - \gamma\delta)[R(t-1)/\gamma b^P(s, t-1) + h(t)] \text{ for all } t \geq s. \tag{5}$$

In equation (5), human wealth (h) is defined as the present value of the disposable-income stream. The relevant discount factor to calculate the present value is the interest rate adjusted by the period-survival factor ($\gamma^j\alpha_j$). By assumption, newcomers and existing cohorts have the same disposable-income stream so that $h(s, t) = h(t)$ for all $s \leq t$. The consumption function for individuals as described in equation (5) is identical to the one in the model with zero population growth and finite horizon. As we shall show next, population growth comes into play, however, when we derive the aggregate consumption function.

Let the "birth rate" ($g \geq 0$) be the same for each cohort, and normalize, without loss of generality, the population size in period 0 to 1: $N(0) = 1$. Population size changes as a result of two factors: the birth or arrival of new generations not connected with previous ones, and the death of existing agents. Combining the implications of these two factors, the size in period 1 of cohorts born in periods 0 and 1 is $N(0, 1) = \gamma$ and $N(1, 1) = g\gamma$, respectively, where $N(s, t)$ denotes the period t size of a cohort born in period s. The size of the total population in period 1 is therefore $N(1) = \gamma + \gamma g = (1 + g)\gamma$, with $N(t)$ denoting period t total population size. Similarly, the population size in period 2 is $\gamma^2 + g\gamma^2 + (g\gamma^2 + g^2\gamma^2) = (1 + g)^2\gamma^2$, and, in any period t: $N(t) = (1 + g)^t\gamma^t$. Total population is therefore growing at a constant rate, $n = [N(t) - N(t-1)]/N(t-1)$:

$$n = (1 + g)\gamma - 1. \tag{6}$$

A high survival probability as well as a high birth rate lead to faster overall population growth.

The constant growth rate of the total population facilitates the derivation of the aggregate consumption path and the laws of motion for financial and human wealth. Per capita aggregates are weighted sums across all cohorts, with the weights depending on a cohort's relative population size. The one-period budget constraints at time t for different cohorts are given by

$c(0, t) + b^P(0, t) = R(t - 1)/\gamma b^P(0, t - 1) + y(t)$ for cohort born at $t = 0$

$c(s, t) + b^P(s, t) = R(t - 1)/\gamma b^P(s, t - 1) + y(t)$ for cohort born at $s < t$

$c(t, t) + b^P(t, t) = R(t - 1)/\gamma b^P(t, t - 1) + y(t)$ for cohort born at t

$$= y(t). \tag{7}$$

The last part of equation (7) reflects that cohorts who join the population have initially no financial assets or debts: $b^P(t, t - 1) = 0$. Aggregating equation (7) across cohorts and dividing by the population size at time t gives the evolution of private per capita debt:

$$B^P(t) = \frac{R(t - 1)}{1 + n} B^P(t - 1) + Y(t) - C(t). \tag{8}$$

In equation (8) and below, per capita aggregates are denoted by capital letters. In a manner similar to the infinite horizon case discussed in exercise IV.7.1, the relevant discount factor for per capita private debt is the rate-of-return on financial assets, R, adjusted by the population growth factor, $1 + n = (1 + g)\gamma$. The latter reflects that newcomers differ from existing populations because they are not endowed with financial assets. The population growth factor also incorporates that there is only a probability, $\gamma \leq 1$, that agents who acquire financial assets in period t survive and enjoy their assets in the subsequent period. But the probability of death affects the evolution of financial wealth only insofar as it has an impact on population growth. This result is the analogue to the case discussed in Frenkel and Razin: If total population size were constant (so that g is zero), financial wealth would have an autoregressive coefficient identical to the world-market interest factor.

All individuals alive in period t receive the same future-income stream and are subject to the same lump-sum taxes. Per capita human wealth at times t and $t - 1$ is thus

$H(t) = h(t)$

$$= y(t) + \gamma \frac{1}{R(t)} y(t + 1) + \gamma^2 \frac{1}{R(t)R(t + 1)} y(t + 2) + \cdots \tag{9a}$$

$H(t - 1) = h(t - 1)$

$$= y(t - 1) + \gamma \frac{1}{R(t - 1)} y(t) + \gamma^2 \frac{1}{R(t - 1)R(t)} y(t + 1) + \cdots. \tag{9b}$$

Combining the two parts of equation (9) gives the law of motion for aggregate per capita human wealth:

$$H(t) = \frac{R(t-1)}{\gamma}[H(t-1) - Y(t-1)]. \tag{10}$$

The relevant interest rate that links per capita human wealth across time is the agent's effective discount rate, that is, the market interest factor R adjusted for the survival probability γ. This contrasts with the financial asset component of wealth, where the effective interest rate incorporates the population growth factor as described in equation (8).

Total per capita wealth is the sum of financial and human wealth. Aggregating across cohorts and dividing by the population size at time t yields $W^p(t) = R(t-1)/(1+n)B^p(t-1) + H(t)$. Using the previously derived laws of motion for per capita private assets and human wealth, and the consumption function (see below), gives the time path for total wealth:

$$W^p(t) = \frac{R(t-1)}{1+n}\gamma\delta W^p(t-1) + \left\{1 - \frac{\gamma}{1+n}\right\}H(t)$$

$$= \frac{R(t-1)}{1+g}\delta W^p(t-1) + \frac{g}{1+g}H(t). \tag{11}$$

A zero birth rate ($g = 0$) is necessary and sufficient for the standard result to reemerge that wealth is proportional across periods with the factor of proportionality depending exclusively on the rate of interest and the agent's time preference. The standard outcome is not invalidated per se by the finiteness of an agent's planning horizon.

Consumption for all cohorts is proportional to their private wealth, the sum of financial and human wealth (see equation 5). The same holds consequently for per capita consumption:

$$C(t) = (1 - \gamma\delta)\left\{\frac{R(t-1)}{1+n}B^p(t-1) + H(t)\right\}$$

$$= (1 - \gamma\delta)W^p(t). \tag{12}$$

The consumption function reflects features of both models: The finiteness of the agent's lifetime affects the agent's savings rate ($\gamma\delta$), while population growth (n) has an impact on the calculation of the per capita value of financial assets. The finite planning horizon has, furthermore, an effect on the relevant discount factor applied in the calculation of the present value of private wealth, as demonstrated in equation (10).

b. To conclude the exercise, we are asked to derive the conditions for Ricardian deficit neutrality. The one-period budget constraint for the domestic government is

$$\tilde{G}(t) + \tilde{B}^g(t) = R(t-1)\tilde{B}^g(t-1) + \tilde{T}(t), \tag{13}$$

where a tilda ($\sim$) denotes the aggregate amount of a government variable, and G, B^g, and T denote total government spending, asset holdings, and tax receipts, respectively. Since the government has an infinite planning horizon, its relevant discount factor is the world-market interest factor, R. To derive the government's budget constraint in per capita terms, we divide equation (13) by the population size in period t. Aggregating across periods and assuming that the solvency condition is satisfied, the government's intertemporal budget constraint at time t can be expressed in terms of *per capita* values as

$$\sum_{j=0}^{\infty} \alpha_j (1+n)^j G(t+j) = \frac{R(t-1)}{1+n} B^g(t-1) + \sum_{j=0}^{\infty} \alpha_j (1+n)^j T(t+j), \tag{14}$$

where G, B^g, and T denote per capita government spending, assets, and taxes, respectively. The relevant discount rate for *per capita* values of the government variables is the interest rate corrected by the population growth rate (n). This contrasts with the private sector where the survival probability affected the discounting of future periods.

Suppose the government institutes a tax cut in period 0 followed by a uniform tax increase in all future periods to maintain government solvency. Assuming a constant interest rate with $R/1+n \leq 1$, and that the government spending path remains unchanged, we can derive the necessary tax adjustments in future periods by differentiating equation (14):

$$dT(0) = -\frac{1}{\dfrac{R}{1+n} - 1} dT. \tag{15}$$

Changes in government tax policies affect private consumption if they alter the value of human wealth, that is, the present value of the disposable income stream. The effects of the temporary tax cut on human wealth can be determined by combining equation (15) with the definition of human wealth for period 0 (compare equation 9). Since lump-sum taxes are by assumption the same for members of all cohorts, the effect of a one-period tax cut on human wealth is

$$\frac{dH(0)}{dT(0)} = -\left\{1 - \frac{\gamma}{1+n}\right\} \frac{R}{R-\gamma}$$

$$= -\left\{1 - \frac{1}{1+g}\right\} \frac{R}{R-\gamma} \leq 0. \tag{16}$$

A tax cut in period 0 followed by compensating tax increases in future periods increases the present value of disposable-income streams if and only if the birth rate is positive: $g > 0$. A finite planning horizon, as in Frenkel and Razin, and positive population growth, as in exercise IV.7.1, are neither necessary nor sufficient to break the Ricardian neutrality position in this more general setting. The rationale for the result stems from differences among groups affected by the tax cut in period 0 and those burdened with future tax liabilities. If no new taxpayers arrive, a temporary tax cut would not relax the private agent's budget constraint. Taxes would shift from the current to future periods, but the present value of taxes for the private consumer would remain unchanged. On the other hand, if new cohorts arrive, the future tax burden would be shared by those new arrivals. The net effect for the current beneficiaries of the tax cut is then a rise in the present value of their disposable income. This would also increase current-period per capita consumption. Combining equations (12) and (16), the effect of a temporary tax cut on period 0 consumption is

$$\frac{dC(0)}{dT(0)} = -(1 - \gamma\delta)\left\{1 - \frac{1}{1+g}\right\} \frac{R}{R-\gamma} \leq 0. \tag{17}$$

The result demonstrates that real allocations are generally not neutral with respect to the timing of lump-sum taxes. The breakdown in the Ricardian neutrality proposition can arise even if agents have infinite planning horizons or if the population growth rate is zero. The critical condition is a positive birth rate of new cohorts, $g > 0$, and other conditions emerge as special cases. In the setup in Frenkel and Razin with finite survival probability, a positive birth rate was implicitly assumed to compensate for the nonunitary survival probability so that total population size remained constant: $g = (1 - \gamma)/\gamma \geq 0$. In the model developed in exercise IV.7.1, cohorts were supposed to have infinite planning horizons so that the population growth rate was identical to the birth rate: $g = n \geq 0$.

8

**An Exposition of
the Two-Country
Overlapping Generations
Model**

Exercise IV.8.1

Consider the two-country overlapping generations model of chapter 8. Suppose that preferences of domestic and foreign agents can be represented by logarithmic utility functions and that the planning horizon is identical for individuals in both countries ($\gamma = \gamma^* < 1$). Let the foreign government's budget be balanced in all periods. Also assume that the path of domestic-government expenditure remains unaffected by the following modifications to the budget deficit:

a. Suppose that all future periods are aggregated into a single period. In this two-period model, derive the effects of an anticipated future budget deficit on the constancy-equivalent interest rate.

b. Let future periods be divided into two separate intervals, a near future and a distant future. Suppose that the domestic government alters taxes in the near future and offsets the revenue effects by changing taxes in the distant future, leaving current-period taxes unchanged. For simplicity assume that initial debt, taxes, and government spending are zero and that outputs are stationary. Show that a deficit in the near future will increase the future interest rate. Also demonstrate that the effect on the interest rate between the current period and the near future depends on a familiar transfer criterion.

Solution

a. In this exercise we are asked to assess the interest effects of budget deficits. The exercise will also illustrate the implications of different forms of time aggregation. First, assume that the future is consolidated into a single period. An anticipated budget deficit in the second period implies a budget surplus in the current period in order for the initial government spending path to be maintained. The effects of an anticipated future budget deficit are thus the mirror image of an unanticipated current budget deficit. Using the results in chapter 8, the constancy-equivalent interest rate will adjust around an initial balanced-budget equilibrium according to

$$\frac{dR}{dT} = (1 - \gamma)\frac{(1 - \gamma\delta)R^2\lambda^*}{\gamma(R - 1)(Y^* - G^*)} > 0, \tag{1}$$

where R is the constancy-equivalent interest, and Y, G, T, and δ denote domestic output, government spending, taxes, and the domestic consumer's discount factor, respectively. An asterisk (*) denotes the corresponding foreign variable, and λ^* is the share of foreign output net of government spending in world output net of government spending. As equation (1) illustrates, a future tax cut ($dT < 0$), which requires a current-period tax hike of $dT_0 = -1/(R - 1)dT$ to ensure government budget balance, will result in a decline in the constancy-equivalent interest rate. The channel is the wealth effect emanating from the current tax increase; it lowers domestic wealth and thereby creates an excess supply of current-period consumption goods. To restore market equilibrium the interest rate must fall.

b. The results in part a are familiar from chapter 8 and serve here as a benchmark to judge the effects of alternative forms of time aggregation. Moreover, they illustrate the limits imposed by two-period aggregation. Since a future tax cut would require an unanticipated tax increase in the current period, two-period aggregation precludes a general discussion of anticipated government deficits and a three-period framework is the minimum setup in this context.

Let time be divided into three periods: period 0, the "present"; period 1, the "near future"; and a representative period after period 1, the "distant future." Equilibrium requires that world demand equals world output in all periods. In addition, domestic and foreign wealth must be equal to the present value of human and financial wealth. Using Walras's law to omit the condition for the distant-future goods market, equilibrium can be described by the following four equations:

$$(1 - \gamma\delta)W_0 + (1 - \gamma\delta^*)W_0^* = (Y_0 - G_0) + (Y_0^* - G_0^*) \tag{2}$$

$$(1 - \gamma\delta)[\gamma\delta R_0 W_0 + (1 - \gamma)H_1] + (1 - \gamma\delta^*)[\gamma\delta^* R_0 W_0^* + (1 - \gamma)H_1^*]$$

$$= (Y_1 - G_1) + (Y_1^* - G_1^*) \tag{3}$$

$$W_0 = (Y_0 - T_0) + \frac{\gamma}{R_0}H_1 + R_{-1}(B_{-1}^g - B_{-1}) \tag{4}$$

$$W_0^* = (Y_0^* - T_0^*) + \frac{\gamma}{R_0}H_1^* + R_{-1}(B_{-1}^{g*} + B_{-1}), \tag{5}$$

where H_1 and H_1^* are the period 1 values of domestic and foreign human wealth, respectively:

$$H_1 = Y_1 - T_1 + \frac{\gamma}{R_1 - \gamma}(Y - T)$$

$$(6)$$

$$H_1^* = Y_1^* - T_1^* + \frac{\gamma}{R_1 - \gamma}(Y^* - T^*).$$

Equation (2) describes the goods-market equilibrium for period 0 and equation (3) the market equilibrium in the near future. The subsequent two equations describe domestic and foreign wealth in period 0 and use the definition of period 1 human wealth in equation (6). Variables without a time subscript refer to the distant future. R_1 denotes the constancy-equivalent interest-rate factor linking the near future with the distant future and distant future periods with each other. Otherwise, the notation is identical to that in chapter 8 of Frenkel and Razin. The equilibrium conditions incorporate that the savings rate with logarithmic utility is $\gamma\delta$.

An anticipated budget deficit in the near future must be followed by rising taxes in the distant future if government expenditures and current-period taxes remain unchanged. Using the government's budget constraint, the size of the distant-future tax increases that offset the near-future tax cut is given by

$$dT = -(R_1 - 1)\,dT_1.$$

$$(7)$$

The effects of an unanticipated tax cut can be found by differentiating equations (2) to (5). Around an initial equilibrium with zero debt, taxes, and government spending, the four endogenous variables adjust according to

$$\frac{dR_0}{dT_1} = \frac{(1 - \gamma)(1 - \gamma\delta)(1 - \gamma\delta^*)\gamma^3 R_1 Y^*}{(R_1 - \gamma)^3 R_0 \Omega}(\gamma\delta - \gamma\delta^*) \gtrless 0$$

$$(8)$$

$$\frac{dR_1}{dT_1} = -\frac{(1 - \gamma)(1 - \gamma\delta)\gamma R_1 \Phi}{(R_1 - \gamma)^2 R_0^2 \Omega} < 0$$

$$(9)$$

$$\frac{dW_0}{dT_1} = -\frac{(1 - \gamma)(1 - \gamma\delta^*)\gamma R_1 Y^*}{[(1 - \gamma\delta)Y + (1 - \gamma\delta^*)Y^*]R_0(R_1 - \gamma)} < 0$$

$$(10)$$

$$\frac{dW_0^*}{dT_1} = \frac{(1 - \gamma)(1 - \gamma\delta)\gamma R_1 Y^*}{[(1 - \gamma\delta)Y + (1 - \gamma\delta^*)Y^*]R_0(R_1 - \gamma)} > 0,$$

$$(11)$$

where

$$\Omega = [(1 - \gamma\delta)Y + (1 - \gamma\delta^*)Y^*]\frac{\gamma^2}{R_0^2(R_1 - \gamma)^2}$$

$$\times \{(1 - \gamma\delta)[\gamma\delta(R_0 R_1 + \gamma R_1 - \gamma R_0) + (1 - \gamma)R_1]Y$$

$$+ (1 - \gamma\delta^*)[\gamma\delta^*(R_0 R_1 + \gamma R_1 - \gamma R_0) + (1 - \gamma)R_1]Y^*\} > 0,$$

and

$$\Phi = (1 - \gamma\delta)[\gamma\delta(R_0 R_1 + \gamma R_1 - \gamma R_0) + (1 - \gamma)R_1]Y$$

$$+ (1 - \gamma\delta^*)[\gamma\delta^*(R_0 R_1 + \gamma R_1 - \gamma R_0) + (1 - \gamma)R_1]Y^* > 0.$$

Equation (9) shows that an anticipated future deficit ($dT_1 < 0$) would raise the constancy-equivalent interest rate. The interpretation is similar to the discussion in section a. A temporary tax cut would increase period 1 wealth of domestic agents as long as these have finite planning horizons ($\gamma < 1$). The positive wealth effect leads to excess demand in the market for period 1 goods, and the interest rate must increase to restore equilibrium; that is, the intertemporal price of period 1 goods must rise.

The effect of an anticipated deficit in the near future on the interest rate in the current period is ambiguous. As equation (8) illustrates, the effect depends on a transfer criterion, the relative savings rate in the domestic and foreign country. The difference in the two savings rates captures whether world wealth ($W_0 + W_0^*$) rises or falls in period 0 in response to the anticipated domestic budget deficit. Foreign wealth will decline since future periods are discounted more heavily as the future interest rate rises. As a result, foreign demand for period 0 goods also declines. Domestic wealth, on the other hand, increases as the effect from future interest rates is more than compensated for by the positive wealth effect stemming from the tax cut in the near future. The rise in domestic wealth will lead to increased domestic demand for period 0 consumption goods. With domestic wealth rising and foreign wealth falling, the aggregate demand effect depends on the relative savings propensities in the two countries. Thus, if the domestic savings propensity exceeds the foreign propensity, the rise in domestic wealth will dominate and world savings will increase. Consequently, world demand for period 0 goods declines and market equilibrium is restored through a fall in period 0 interest rates, that is, a decline in the intertemporal price of goods in period 0. On the other hand, if ($\gamma\delta - \gamma\delta^*$) < 0 so that the foreign saving propensity exceeds the domestic propensity to save, world savings will tend to fall in the current period. The decline in world saving will lead to a rise in interest rates, restoring market equilibrium in the current period.

Exercise IV.8.2[1]

Consider a small open-economy version of the model in chapter 8. Suppose that the country produces both tradable and nontradable goods and that the output levels of either good are fixed over time. Agents have a finite planning horizon as a result of their finite lifespan and incomplete bequest motives. Also assume that the consumer's preferences can be represented by a logarithmic expected-utility function. The government buys tradable and nontradable goods and its purchases are financed with lump-sum taxes. Finally, assume that the small country faces a constant interest rate, r_x, in terms of the tradable good, the numeraire in the analysis.
a. Show that the private propensity to save is independent of the real exchange rate.
b. Suppose that the government implements an unanticipated tax cut in the current period followed by a tax increase in the subsequent period leaving government spending patterns unchanged. Prove that the unanticipated current-period tax cut leads to an increase in today's nontradable-goods price and a lower nontradable-goods price in the next period. Also describe the effects of the unanticipated deficit on consumption and the economy's external debt.

Solution

a. Temporal preferences are defined over two goods, consumption of tradables (c_{xt}) and nontradables (c_{mt}). Assuming that the subutility function over the two goods is linear homogeneous, the problem can be modelled as a two-step decision problem. First, allocate consumption among goods in period t (temporal problem), and, second, allocate spending across periods (intertemporal problem). Let $c_t(c_{xt}, c_{mt})$ denote total consumption in period t and $P_t(p_{nt})$ the corresponding utility-based price index, where p_{nt} is the price of the nontradable good in period t in terms of tradables (the inverse of the real exchange rate). Total spending in period t is $z_t = P_t C_t = c_{xt} + p_{nt} c_{mt}$. The individual consumer maximizes the certainty-equivalence form of his expected-utility function subject to the intertemporal budget constraint:

$$\max \sum_{v=0}^{\infty} (\gamma\delta)^v \ln(c_{t+v}) \tag{1}$$

---

1. This exercise is based on chapter 13 in [19].

subject to

$$\sum_{v=0}^{\infty} \left(\frac{\gamma}{R}\right)^{v} P_{t+v} c_{t+v} = \sum_{v=0}^{\infty} \left(\frac{\gamma}{R}\right)^{v} [\bar{y}_x + p_{n,t+v} \bar{y}_n - T_{t+v}] - \frac{R}{\gamma} b_{s,t-1}$$

$$\equiv w_{s,t}.$$

The period-survival probability is denoted by γ ($\gamma \leq 1$), taxes by T, and R is the world interest factor, which is constant by assumption. In specifying the budget constraint it was assumed that the consumer's solvency condition is satisfied so that a consumer born in period s is able to repay his personal debt: $\lim_{v \to \infty} \gamma^{v} \alpha_{v} b_{s,t+v} = 0$, where $b_{s,t+v}$ denotes time $- (t + v)$ financial debt of a consumer born in period s. Financial debt instruments form part of the consumer's wealth, $w(s, t)$, which also includes endowment incomes of tradable ($\bar{y}_x$) and nontradable goods ($\bar{y}_n$). The solution to the decision problem in equation (1) yields the individual's consumption function. For logarithmic utility, consumption in period t of an agent born at time s is proportional to wealth:

$$c_{s,t} = (1 - \gamma\delta) w_{s,t}. \tag{2a}$$

Since the same holds for agents of all cohorts s in period t, aggregate per capita consumption is proportional to aggregate per capita wealth,

$$C_t = (1 - \gamma\delta) W_t, \tag{2b}$$

where capital letters denote aggregate per capita values. The savings rate, $\gamma\delta$, is independent of the real exchange rate when preferences are logarithmic with linear homogeneous subutility functions.

b. To assess the effects of a tax cut we first derive exact solutions for the time profile of the real exchange rate and private debt. The reader who is not interested in the technical details can skip the following derivations and turn directly to the subsequent discussion of the government deficit.

Aggregating individual wealth as specified in equation (1) across cohorts yields per capita aggregate wealth:

$$W(t) = \frac{R}{R - \gamma} \bar{Y}_x + \sum_{v=0}^{\infty} \left(\frac{\gamma}{R}\right)^{v} \{p_{n,t+v} \bar{Y}_n - T_{t+v}\} - RB_{t-1}^{p}. \tag{3}$$

Consider an initial equilibrium with zero government spending. Equilibrium in the nontradable-goods market requires then that private domestic demand equal the supply of nontradables:

$$(1 - \gamma\delta) \beta_n W_t = p_{nt} \bar{Y}_n. \tag{4}$$

where β_n denotes the expenditure share of nontradables and is constant given our restrictions on consumer preferences. The evolution of private debt can be derived from the aggregate per capita budget constraint. Using the definition of the expenditure share, β_n, to substitute for the consumption demand of tradables and applying the market-clearing condition for nontradables yields

$$B_t^p = RB_{t-1}^p + \frac{1 - \beta_n}{\beta_n} p_{nt} \overline{Y}_n - \overline{Y}_x + T_t. \tag{5}$$

The model is closed by the aggregate solvency condition $\lim_{v \to \infty} (1/R)^v B_v^p = 0$. For notational convenience we denote the savings rate by s ($s \equiv \gamma\delta$) and the discounted sum of the values of future nontradable outputs by Q_{nt}:

$$Q_{nt} \equiv \sum_{v=0}^{\infty} \left(\frac{\gamma}{R}\right)^v p_{n,t+1+v} \overline{Y}_n, \quad \text{and} \quad Q_{n,t-1} = p_{nt} \overline{Y}_n + \frac{\gamma}{R} Q_{nt}. \tag{6}$$

Substituting these definitions into equations (4) and (5) and combining the results yields the evolution of the discounted sum of future outputs:

$$Q_{nt} = \frac{R}{\gamma} \left\{ [1 - (1 - s)\beta_n]Q_{n,t-1} - (1 - s)\beta_n \frac{R}{R - \gamma} \overline{Y}_x \right.$$
$$\left. + (1 - s)\beta_n \sum_{v=0}^{\infty} \left(\frac{\gamma}{R}\right)^v T_{t+v} + (1 - s)\beta_n RB_{t-1}^p \right\}. \tag{7}$$

Using similar substitutions yields the dynamics of private debt:

$$B_t^p = RB_{t-1}^p + \frac{1 - \beta_n}{\beta_n} \left(Q_{n,t-1} - \frac{\gamma}{R} Q_{nt} \right) - (\overline{Y}_x - T_t). \tag{8}$$

Substituting for Q_{nt} from equation (7) we can rewrite equation (8) as

$$B_t^p = [1 - (1 - s)(1 - \beta_n)]RB_{t-1}^p + (1 - s)(1 - \beta_n)Q_{n,t-1}$$
$$- \left(1 - (1 - s)(1 - \beta_n) \frac{R}{R - \gamma} \right) \overline{Y}_x + T_t$$
$$- (1 - s)(1 - \beta_n) \sum_{v=0}^{\infty} \left(\frac{\gamma}{R}\right)^v T_{t+v}. \tag{9}$$

Equations (7) and (9) can be expressed in a matrix form as follows:

$$\begin{pmatrix} Q_{nt} \\ B_t^p \end{pmatrix} = A \begin{pmatrix} Q_{n,t-1} \\ B_{t-1}^p \end{pmatrix} + a\overline{Y}_x + D_t, \tag{10}$$

where

$$A = \begin{bmatrix} [1 - (1 - s)\beta_n]\dfrac{R}{\gamma} & (1 - s)\beta_n\dfrac{R^2}{\gamma} \\ (1 - \beta_n)(1 - s) & [1 - (1 - \beta_n)(1 - s)]R \end{bmatrix},$$

$$a = \begin{bmatrix} -\dfrac{\beta_n(1 - s)R^2}{\gamma(R - \gamma)} \\ (1 - \beta_n)(1 - s)\dfrac{R}{R - \gamma} - 1 \end{bmatrix},$$

and

$$D_t = \begin{bmatrix} \dfrac{(1 - s)\beta_n R}{\gamma} \sum_{v=0}^{\infty} \left(\dfrac{\gamma}{R}\right)^v T_{t+v} \\ T_t - (1 - \beta_n)(1 - s) \sum_{v=0}^{\infty} \left(\dfrac{\gamma}{R}\right)^v T_{t+v} \end{bmatrix}.$$

We first solve the system of equation (10) for the case in which there are no taxes. Accordingly, the solution is

$$\begin{pmatrix} Q_{nt} \\ B_t^p \end{pmatrix} = \overline{Y}_x(I - A)^{-1}a + A^{t+1}\begin{pmatrix} Q_{n,-1} \\ B_{-1}^p \end{pmatrix}, \tag{11}$$

where I is the identity matrix. The first expression on the righthand side of equation (11) is

$$\begin{pmatrix} Q \\ B^p \end{pmatrix} \equiv \overline{Y}_x(I - A)^{-1}a = -\frac{\overline{Y}_x}{\Delta}\begin{bmatrix} \dfrac{\beta_n(1 - s)(1 - \gamma)R^2}{\gamma(R - \gamma)} \\ 1 - \delta R \end{bmatrix}, \tag{12}$$

where

$$\Delta = \frac{1}{\gamma}[\beta_n R(1 - s)(1 - \gamma) - (1 - sR)(R - \gamma)].$$

To compute the second expression on the righthand side of (11), we recall from the rules of matrix algebra that

$$A^{t+1} = V\Omega^{t+1}V^{-1}, \tag{13}$$

where Ω is the diagonal matrix with the eigenvalues of A on its diagonal and V is the matrix of the corresponding eigenvectors. That is,

$$\Omega = \begin{pmatrix} \lambda_1 & 0 \\ 0 & \lambda_2 \end{pmatrix} \quad \text{and} \quad V = \begin{pmatrix} v_1 & v_2 \\ 1 & 1 \end{pmatrix},$$

where we have normalized the second component of each of the eigenvectors to unity. Computing the expressions for the eigenvalues of A yields

$$\lambda_i = \frac{R}{2}[\mu + (-1)^i\sqrt{\mu^2 - 4\delta}], \quad i = 1, 2, \tag{14}$$

where

$$\mu = (1 - \beta_n)\left(\frac{1}{\gamma} + s\right) + \beta_n(1 + \delta).$$

Similarly, the first components of the eigenvectors in V are

$$v_i = \frac{\lambda_i - R[1 - (1 - \beta_n)(1 - s)]}{(1 - \beta_n)(1 - s)}, \quad i = 1, 2. \tag{15}$$

Now that we have the expressions for the matrices Ω and V, we can compute A^{t+1} in equation (12). Substituting the resulting expression along with equation (12) into equation (11) yields

$$Q_{nt} = Q + \frac{1}{v_2 - v_1}\{[v_2(Q_{n,-1} - Q) - v_1 v_2(B^p_{-1} - B^p)]\lambda_2^{t+1}$$

$$- [v_1(Q_{n,-1} - Q) - v_1 v_2(B^p_{-1} - B^p)]\lambda_1^{t+1}\}, \tag{16}$$

$$B^p_t = B^p + \frac{1}{v_2 - v_1}\{[Q_{n,-1} - Q) - v_1(B^p_{-1} - B^p)]\lambda_1^{t+1}$$

$$- [(Q_{n,-1} - Q) - v_2(B^p_{-1} - B^p)]\lambda_2^{t+1}\}. \tag{17}$$

Observing from (14) that $\lambda_2 > R$ and applying the solvency condition to equation (17) yields the restriction

$$Q_{n,-1} = Q + v_1(B^p_{-1} - B^p). \tag{18}$$

This restriction nails down the initial value of $Q_{n,-1}$, and from equation (6) it also determines the initial value of $p_{n_0}\overline{Y}_n$. Substituting equation (18) into equations (16) and (17) yields

$$Q_{nt} = Q + v_1(B^p_{-1} - B^p)\lambda_1^{t+1}, \tag{19}$$

$$B^p_t = B^p + (B^p_{-1} - B^p)\lambda_1^{t+1}. \tag{20}$$

Finally, to obtain the solution for $p_{nt} \bar{Y}_n$, we substitute equations (19) and (20) into equation (6). Accordingly,

$$p_{nt} = \frac{1}{\bar{Y}_n}\left[\frac{R-\gamma}{R}Q + \left(\frac{R-\lambda_1\gamma}{R}\right)v_1(B^p_{-1} - B^p)\lambda_1^t\right]$$

$$= \bar{p}_n + \bar{v}(B^p_{-1} - B)\lambda_1^t. \tag{21}$$

Equations (19) and (20), or alternatively (20) and (21), constitute the solution to the system ((10) for the case in which there are no taxes ($D_t = 0$). As is evident, since $\lambda_1 < 1$, the condition for the existence of steady-state equilibrium is that $Q > 0$. Using equation (12), this condition requires that $\beta_n R(1 - \gamma\delta)(1 - \gamma) < (1 - \gamma\delta R)(R - \gamma)$. For example, if $\gamma\delta R < 1$ and $\beta_n < (1 - \gamma\delta R)(R - \gamma)/(1 - \gamma\delta)(1 - \gamma)$, then the steady state exists. Likewise, if R approaches unity, then the steady-state equilibrium also exists. In the steady state the country is a net debtor if $1 > \delta R$, and vice versa.

We turn next to develop a procedure of solving the system shown in equation (11) for the case in which the government follows a tax policy so that $D_t \neq 0$.

Assume now that the government raises period 0 taxes by the amount T. To balance its intertemporal budget, future taxes must be lowered. Suppose that in period 1 taxes are lowered by the amount RT, whereas in all other periods they are set at zero. This tax structure is then applied to equation (10) to get the general solution of the equilibrium system.

The time-dependent vector D_t in equation (10) is

$$D_0 = \begin{bmatrix} D_0^1 \\ D_0^2 \end{bmatrix} = \begin{bmatrix} \dfrac{R}{\gamma}\beta_n(1-s)(1-\gamma) \\ [1-(1-\beta_n)(1-s)(1-\gamma)] \end{bmatrix} \cdot T,$$

$$D_1 = \begin{bmatrix} D_1^1 \\ D_1^2 \end{bmatrix} = \begin{bmatrix} -\dfrac{R^2}{\gamma}\beta_n(1-s) \\ -R[1-(1-\beta_n)(1-s)] \end{bmatrix} \cdot T, \tag{22}$$

and

$$D_t = 0, \, t = 2, 3, \ldots.$$

Since from period 2 onward taxes are zero, we can apply the solution stated in equations (19) and (20) to this period for any given value of B_1^p. An equation of the type shown in (18) implies that there is a corresponding equilibrium value Q_{n1}. Accordingly,

$$Q_{n1} = Q + v_1(B_1^p - B^p). \tag{23}$$

We now iterate backward, using equations (10) and (22) to find the general-equilibrium path for the initially given value of debt B_{-1}^p. Rearranging (10) yields

$$\begin{bmatrix} Q_{n0} \\ B_0^p \end{bmatrix} = \begin{bmatrix} A^{11}(Q_{n1} - a_1\overline{Y}_x - D_1^1) + A^{12}(B_1^p - a_2\overline{Y}_x - D_1^2) \\ A^{21}(Q_{n1} - a_1\overline{Y}_x - D_1^1) + A^{22}(B_1^p - a_2\overline{Y}_x - D_1^2) \end{bmatrix}, \tag{24}$$

$$\begin{bmatrix} Q_{n,-1} \\ B_{-1}^p \end{bmatrix} = \begin{bmatrix} A^{11}(Q_{n0} - a_1\overline{Y}_x - D_0^1) + A^{12}(B_0^p - a_2\overline{Y}_x - D_0^2) \\ A^{21}(Q_{n0} - a_1\overline{Y}_x - D_0^1) + A^{22}(B_0^p - a_2\overline{Y}_x - D_0^2) \end{bmatrix}, \tag{25}$$

where A^{ij} is the ijth component of the inverse of the A matrix and a_i is the ith component of the a vector. Expressed explicitly, using $s = \gamma\delta$, these terms are

$$A^{11} = \frac{1}{\delta R}[1 - (1 - \beta_n)(1 - \gamma\delta)] > 0,$$

$$A^{12} = -\frac{(1 - \gamma\delta)}{\gamma\delta}\beta_n < 0,$$

$$A^{21} = -\frac{1}{\delta R^2}(1 - \beta_n)(1 - \gamma\delta) < 0, \tag{26}$$

$$A^{22} = \frac{1}{\gamma\delta R}[1 - \beta_n(1 - \gamma\delta)] > 0,$$

$$a_1 = -\frac{R^2\beta_n(1 - \gamma\delta)}{(R - \gamma)\gamma} < 0,$$

$$a_2 = \frac{R}{R - \gamma}(1 - \beta_n)(1 - \gamma\delta) - 1,$$

where it is noted that $A^{11} > \gamma/R$.

Solving for (Q_{n0}, B_0^p) and substituting the resulting solutions into (25) yields

$$Q_{n,-1} = M + [A^{11}(A^{11}v_1 + A^{12}) + A^{12}(A^{21}v_1 + A^{22})]B_1^p$$

$$- (1 - \gamma)\frac{(1 - \gamma\delta)\beta_n}{\gamma\delta}T, \tag{27}$$

where

$$M = A^{11}[A^{11}(Q - v_1 B^p - a_1 \overline{Y}_x) - A^{12}a_2 \overline{Y}_x - a_1 \overline{Y}_x]$$
$$+ A^{12}[A^{21}(Q - v_1 B^p - a_1 \overline{Y}_x) - A^{22}a_2 \overline{Y}_x - a_2 \overline{Y}_x],$$

and

$$B^p_{-1} = N + [A^{21}(A^{11}v_1 + A^{12}) + A^{22}(A^{21}v_1 + A^{22})]B^p_1$$

$$+ (1 - \gamma)\frac{1}{\gamma\delta R}(1 - \beta_n)(1 - \gamma\delta)T, \qquad (28)$$

where

$$N = A^{21}[A^{11}(Q - v_1 B^p - a_1 \overline{Y}_x) - A^{12}a_2 \overline{Y}_x - a_1 \overline{Y}_x]$$
$$+ A^{22}[A^{21}(Q - v_1 B^p - a_1 \overline{Y}_x) - A^{22}a_2 \overline{Y}_x - a_2 \overline{Y}_x].$$

Solving for B^p_1 from equation (28) and substituting the result into equations (27), (23), and (24) yields

$$Q_{n,-1} = M - \frac{A^{11}(A^{11}v_1 + A^{12}) + A^{12}(A^{21}v_1 + A^{22})}{A^{21}(A^{11}v_1 + A^{12}) + A^{22}(A^{21}v_1 + A^{22})}N$$

$$+ \frac{A^{11}(A^{11}v_1 + A^{12}) + A^{12}(A^{21}v_1 + A^{22})}{A^{21}(A^{11}v_1 + A^{12}) + A^{22}(A^{21}v_1 + A^{22})}B^p_{-1}$$

$$- (1 - \gamma)\frac{(1 - \gamma\delta)}{\gamma\delta R}$$

$$\times \left[\frac{A^{11}(A^{11}v_1 + A^{12}) + A^{12}(A^{21}v_1 + A^{22})}{A^{21}(A^{11}v_1 + A^{12}) + A^{22}(A^{21}v_1 + A^{22})}\right.$$

$$\left. \times (1 - \beta_n) - R\beta_n\right]T. \qquad (29)$$

$$Q_{n0} = A^{11}(Q - v_1 B^p - a_1 \overline{Y}_x) - A^{12}a_2 \overline{Y}_x$$

$$- \frac{A^{11}v_1 + A^{12}}{A^{21}(A^{11}v_1 + A^{12}) + A^{22}(A^{21}v_1 + A^{22})}N$$

$$+ \left[\frac{A^{11}v_1 + A^{12}}{A^{21}(A^{11}v_1 + A^{12}) + A^{22}(A^{21}v_1 + A^{22})}\right]B^p_{-1}$$

$$- (1 - \gamma)\frac{(1 - \beta_n)(1 - \gamma\delta)}{\gamma\delta R}$$

$$\times \left[\frac{A^{11}v_1 + A^{12}}{A^{21}(A^{11}v_1 + A^{12}) + A^{22}(A^{21}v_1 + A^{22})}\right]T, \qquad (30)$$

$$Q_{n1} = \left[Q - v_1 B^p - \frac{v_1 N}{A^{21}(A^{11}v_1 + A^{12}) + A^{22}(A^{21}v_1 + A^{22})} \right]$$

$$+ \left[\frac{v_1}{A^{21}(A^{11}v_1 + A^{12}) + A^{22}(A^{21}v_1 + A^{22})} \right] B^p_{-1}$$

$$- (1 - \gamma) \frac{(1 - \beta_n)(1 - \gamma\delta)}{\gamma\delta R}$$

$$\times \left[\frac{v_1}{A^{21}(A^{11}v_1 + A^{12}) + A^{22}(A^{21}v_1 + A^{22})} \right] T, \tag{31}$$

where it is noted from the previous expressions that the backeted terms multiplying T in equations (30) and (31) are negative.

We are now in a position to calculate the equilibrium values of the output of nontradable goods. Using equations (6) and (29) through (31) yields

$$p_{no} \bar{Y}_n = P_0$$

$$+ \left[\frac{A^{11}(A^{11}v_1 + A^{12}) + A^{12}(A^{21}v_1 + A^{22}) - \gamma/R(A^{11}v_1 + A^{12})}{A^{21}(A^{11}v_1 + A^{12}) + A^{22}(A^{21}v_1 + A^{22})} \right] B^p_{-1}$$

$$- \frac{(1 - \gamma)(1 - \gamma\delta)}{\gamma\delta R}$$

$$\times \left\{ \frac{[A^{11} - (\gamma/R)](A^{11}v_1 + A^{12}) + A^{12}(A^{21}v_1 + A^{22})}{A^{21}(A^{11}v_1 + A^{12}) + A^{22}(A^{21}v_1 + A^{22})} \right.$$

$$\times (1 - \beta_n) - R\beta_n \bigg\} T, \tag{32}$$

where

$$P_0 = M - \frac{N\{[A^{11} - (\gamma/R)](A^{11}v_1 + A^{12}) + A^{12}(A^{21}v_1 + A^{22})\}}{A^{21}(A^{11}v_1 + A^{12}) + A^{22}(A^{21}v_1 + A^{22})}$$

$$- \frac{\gamma}{R}[A^{11}(Q - v_1 B^p - a_1 \bar{Y}_x) - A^{12}a_2 \bar{Y}_x],$$

and

$$p_{n1}\,\overline{Y}_n = P_1 + \left[\frac{A^{11}v_1 + A^{12} - \gamma v_1/R}{A^{21}(A^{11}v_1 + A^{12}) + A^{22}(A^{21}v_1 + A^{22})}\right]B^p_{-1}$$

$$- (1 - \gamma)\frac{(1 - \beta_n)(1 - \gamma\delta)}{\gamma\delta R}$$

$$\times \left[\frac{A^{11}v_1 + A^{12} - \gamma v_1/R}{A^{21}(A^{11}v_1 + A^{12}) + A^{22}(A^{21}v_1 + A^{22})}\right]T, \qquad (33)$$

where

$$P_1 = A^{11}(Q - v_1 B^p - a_1 \overline{Y}_x) - A^{12}a_2 \overline{Y}_x - \frac{\gamma}{R}(Q - v_1 B^p)$$

$$- \frac{H[A^{11}v_1 + A^{12} - (\gamma/R)v_1]}{A^{21}(A^{11}v_1 + A^{12}) + A^{22}(A^{21}v_1 + A^{22})}.$$

To sign the tax coefficients one can use equations (10), (12), (14), and (15), and the fact that $A^{11} > \gamma/R$ and $v_1 < 0$. Together, these conditions imply that the tax coefficients in equations (32) and (33) are negative and positive, respectively. A budget deficit, arising from a current-period tax cut and an offsetting tax hike in the following period ($T < 0$), raises the current-period price of nontradables, p_{n0}, but lowers the price of non-tradables in the following period. By using equations (19) and (28), it is straightforward to show that all future prices of nontradables would decline. But the more distant the budget maneuvers in periods 0 and 1 become, the smaller the effect will be and, asymptotically, p_{nt} reverts to its original value.

The economic rationale behind the results stems from the wealth effects of budget deficits in the finite horizon model with constant population size. The combined effect of a tax cut in period 0 and a rise in period 1 to restore budget balance is an increase in private-sector wealth in period 0. The rise in wealth leads to higher consumption demand in period 0, including the demand for nontradables. To restore market equilibrium for nontradable goods, their relative price must rise as illustrated by the market-clearing condition in equation (4). In period 1, all agents are burdened with the higher tax liability that is required to offset the initial tax cut. As a result of the tax increase, wealth of agents born in period t declines. Agents born before period 1 benefited from the tax cut and were able to increase their financial wealth, but they also spent part of the tax relief in period 0. As a result, aggregate private wealth declines in period 1 relative to the level that would have been obtained in the absence of the budgetary adjustments. To restore equilibrium in the market for nontradable goods, the decline in aggregate wealth must be accompanied by a decline in their relative price; that is, the real exchange rate must rise. Agents born after period 1 are not directly affected by the changes in tax policies in periods 0 and 1. As the weight of these generations increases over time, the effects of the temporary budget deficit dissipates. Consequently, the relative price of nontradable goods, after falling in period 1, would gradually increase over time and revert to the original path.

Assuming that government debt is initially zero, aggregate private debt will be identical to external debt except for periods in which tax adjustments take place. When the tax cut occurs in period 0, government debt increases. At the same time private debt decreases, but since the private sector spends part of the reduced tax burden on additional consumption, the economy's aggregate debt position deteriorates. In period 1, the government retires its debt and the country's external debt position becomes again identical to private-sector debt. Since the private sector spent part of the tax cut on increased consumption in period 0, the net effect of the temporary tax cut is a deterioration in private-sector debt at the end of period 1. The provisions taken in period 0 were insufficient to retire the public debt in full in period 1 and restore the original foreign debt pattern. Over time the share of agents affected by the tax cut becomes progressively smaller as a result of their finite lifetimes. Consequently, private debt and, thereby, external indebtedness return asymptotically to their original levels.

Exercise IV.8.3

Consider a monetary version of the model in chapter 8. Assume that domestic and foreign goods are internationally tradable and perfect substitutes. At the *beginning* of each period financial markets are open and agents acquire their desired asset portfolios. As part of these transactions they purchase domestic and foreign currencies based on their planned consumption purchases *during* the period, that is, at a time when the financial markets are closed. Accordingly, goods purchases are subject to a cash-in-advance constraint. It is assumed that cash payments have to be conducted in terms of the seller's country's currency. At the end of each period, which is equivalent to the beginning of the next period, domestic firms redistribute their receipts to domestic residents and foreign firms to foreign residents. For simplicity, assume that the domestic country pegs its exchange rate at a unified level for all transactions and faces a given interest rate and price level in terms of the foreign currency. As in chapter 8, individuals have finite lives with a constant probability of survival (γ), and their preferences are characterized by a logarithmic expected-utility function.

a. Describe the equilibria in the goods and asset markets.

b. Show that exchange-rate interventions affect the individual's wealth (for $\gamma < 1$) and thereby the consumption opportunity set, but leave intertemporal prices unchanged. Thus, one can interpret exchange-rate management as a lump-sum tax policy.

Solution

a. At the beginning of each period agents use their resources to acquire domestic and foreign currencies and financial assets. The budget constraint in period t for a domestic agent born at time s is

$$m_h(s, t) + em_f(s, t) - b_h^p(s, t) - eb_f^p(s, t)$$

$$= P(t-1)Y_x(t-1) - T(t) - \frac{R(t-1)}{\gamma}\{b_h^p(s, t-1) + eb_f^p(s, t-1)\}.$$

(1)

In equation (1), $m(s, t)$ and $b(s, t)$ denote currency purchases and financial debt acquisitions, respectively, at time t of an agent born at time s. $T(t)$ is the domestic agent's tax burden. A subscript $i = h, f$ refers to the home or foreign country, e is the exchange rate, and $P(t-1)Y_x(t-1)$ denotes domestic dividends, which are based on the sales in the previous period. Equation (1) assumes that the interest-parity condition holds so that returns on domestic (b_h) and foreign (b_f) assets are equalized. During the period agents can apply their holdings of domestic and foreign currency to the purchase of domestic and foreign consumption goods subject to the following cash-in-advance constraints:

$$P(t)c_x(s, t) \leq m_h(s, t)$$

(2)

$$P^*(t)c_m(s, t) \leq m_f(s, t).$$

(3)

In equations (2) and (3) it is assumed that sales are undertaken in the seller's currency so that, for example, purchases of importable goods require the foreign country's currency. With a positive nominal interest rate (R), money will be held only for transaction purposes and the cash-in-advance constraints will be strictly binding. Assuming also that the purchasing-power-parity condition holds ($eP^* = P$) and that the agent's solvency condition is satisfied, one can combine the temporal budget constraints and the cash-in-advance constraints to derive the agent's intertemporal budget constraint:

$$\sum_{j=0}^{\infty} \left(\frac{\gamma}{R}\right)^j c(s, t + j) = \sum_{j=0}^{\infty} \left(\frac{\gamma}{R}\right)^j \{Y_x(t - 1 + j) - T(t + j)\}$$

$$- \frac{R(t - 1)}{\gamma} b^p(s, t - 1)$$

$$\equiv w(s, t). \tag{4}$$

Equation (4) defines individual wealth ($w(s, t)$) as the sum of the present value of dividends, net of taxes, and the beginning-of-period financial debt. In deriving the intertemporal budget constraint, the exchange rate and the foreign price of the consumption good were normalized to unity. The foreign interest rate was assumed to be constant and b^p denotes the sum of domestic and foreign debt: $b^p = b_h^p + b_f^p$.

To assess the role of monetary policy in this model we begin by specifying the government-sector budget constraint. For simplicity assume that the government's activities are exclusively related to the support of the exchange-rate system. It is convenient to divide these activities into two types of transactions. In the first type, which involves domestic currency, the government sector uses taxes and domestic currency creation ($D(t)$) to finance its purchases of foreign exchange:

$$X(t) = T(t) + D(t), \tag{5}$$

where $X(t)$ denotes the domestic-currency value of the government's foreign exchange outlays. Since $D(t)$ is the net increase of the domestic currency in period t, one can use equation (5) to describe the evolution of the stock of domestic money (M) in terms of foreign-exchange interventions and taxes:

$$M(t) = M(t - 1) + D(t) \tag{6}$$

$$= M(t - 1) + X(t) - T(t).$$

A second type of government activity applies the amount raised in the domestic market to finance any balance-of-payments shortfalls or to absorb balance-of-payments surpluses in order to support the fixed exchange rate. Therefore, the amount $X(t)$ closes the gap between the issue of new and the retirement of old one-period external debt of the government sector (B_f^g):

$$R(t - 1)B_f^g(t - 1) = B_f^g(t) + X(t). \tag{7}$$

The relationship between $X(t)$ and the balance of payments becomes clearer when we use the equilibrium conditions for the trade balance (TA), service (SA), and capital (KA) accounts:

$$TA(t) = C_x^*(t) - C_m(t) = M_h^*(t) - M_f(t) \tag{8a}$$

$$SA(t) = [R(t-1) - 1][B_h^{*p}(t-1) - B_f^p(t-1)] \tag{8b}$$

$$KA(t) = [B_f^p(t) - B_f^p(t-1)] - [B_h^{*p}(t) - B_h^{*p}(t-1)]. \tag{8c}$$

An asterisk (*) refers to a foreign agent's variable, and capital letters denote aggregate per capita values. Combining equations (8a)–(8c) and using the results in equation (7) yields

$$X(t) = TA(t) + SA(t) + KA(t). \tag{9}$$

The government's net purchases in support of the exchange rate, $X(t)$, are the sum of the three private-sector accounts of the balance of payments and thus capture the change in foreign reserves in the home country.

b. To assess the effects of exchange-rate interventions it will be useful first to aggregate the individuals' budget constraints described in equation (4) into an aggregate per capita budget constraint. Employing the cash-in-advance constraints, one can substitute $M(t-1)$ for $Y_x(t-1)$. Moreover, one can use equation (6) and express taxes in terms of money stocks and foreign-exchange interventions. Following otherwise familiar steps of aggregation across cohorts, per capita equilibrium wealth in period t is

$$W(t) = \sum_{j=0}^{\infty} \left(\frac{\gamma}{R}\right)^j Y_x(t+j) - \sum_{j=0}^{\infty} \left(\frac{\gamma}{R}\right)^j X(t+j) - R(t-1)B^p(t-1). \tag{10}$$

Equation (10) displays the familiar result that the effective discount rates applicable to financial and human wealth are different if the agent's lifetime is finite. The effective interest rate applicable to foreign-exchange-rate interventions is the same as for dividend incomes.

The relationship between the government's financing path and private wealth can be made explicit by substituting for $X(t)$ the value of aggregate debt of the domestic economy. Employing the definition of aggregate debt $(B = B^g + B^p)$ and using equation (7) yields

$$\sum_{j=0}^{\infty} \left(\frac{\gamma}{R}\right)^j X(t+j) = \sum_{j=0}^{\infty} \left(\frac{\gamma}{R}\right)^j \{R(t-1+j)B_f^g(t-1+j) - B_f^g(t+j)\}$$

$$= -(1-\gamma) \sum_{j=0}^{\infty} \left(\frac{\gamma}{R}\right)^j \{B(t+j) - B^p(t+j)\}$$

$$+ R(t-1)B^g(t-1) \tag{11}$$

where we used the assumption that all government-sector debt is external debt. Finally, substituting the results of equation (11) into equation (10) yields per capita private wealth as a function of the present value of dividends, the government's debt profile, and the initial external debt position of the domestic economy. In equilibrium, per capita wealth will be identical to the present value of consumption:

$$\sum_{j=0}^{\infty} \left(\frac{\gamma}{R}\right)^j C(t+j) = \sum_{j=0}^{\infty} \left(\frac{\gamma}{R}\right)^j Y_x(t+j) + (1-\gamma) \sum_{j=0}^{\infty} \left(\frac{\gamma}{R}\right)^j B^g(t+j)$$

$$- R(t-1)B(t-1)$$

$$= W(t). \tag{12}$$

Equation (12) demonstrates that the intertemporal profile of government debt has implications for private-sector wealth as long as the lifetime of agents is finite ($\gamma < 1$). In our model, with no government goods purchases the time profile of government debt is determined by interventions in support of the fixed-exchange-rate regime. And unless taxes are designed to offset any change in the demand for money, variations in money demand will require interventions in the foreign-exchange market. Since these actions are reflected in foreign reserve changes and in the government's debt profile, exchange-rate interventions affect private-sector wealth. Moreover, wealth effects are the only distortions introduced by the management of the fixed-exchange-rate system. The intertemporal price of consumption remains unaffected as can be inferred from the agent's budget constraint in equation (12).

Consumption is proportional to wealth for logarithmic preferences with the familiar property that the savings rate is the product of survival probability and the individual's discount factor: $C(t) = (1 - \gamma\delta)W(t)$. Comparing the results in this monetary model with those of the real model in Frenkel and Razin, management of a fixed-exchange-rate regime generates the same real effects as a system of lump-sum taxes and transfers. Both influence consumer behavior through wealth effects but introduce no intertemporal distortions into the system and, in particular, do not affect intertemporal goods prices.

References for Part IV: [2], [3], [4], [8], [19], [22], [25], [49].

V

Distortionary Tax Incentives: Concepts and Applications

9

Equivalence Relations in International Taxation[1]

Exercise V.9.1

Consider a two-country, two-period stock market model. In the first period agents allocate their initial wealth among three assets: a riskless bond offering a return (R), a domestic equity offering an uncertain return (R_1), and foreign equity with stochastic return (R_2). Aside from the equity returns, domestic and foreign taxes form a second source of uncertainty. These are levelled on dividends from equity holdings in the second period with tax rates based on the country of residence of the investor (destination or residence principle).

For simplicity, suppose that consumption of a single consumer good is confined to the second period. Also assume that the agent's expected-utility function can be represented by a mean-variance preference function:

$$E\{V_h\} - \frac{1}{2\tau_h}\mathrm{Var}\{V_h\},$$

where E denotes the expectations operator, Var the variance, and V_h the home country's after-tax return on its portfolio. A similar function characterizes the foreign consumer's preferences. The parameter τ_j ($j = h, f$ and $\tau_j > 0$) may differ across countries and is a measure of the agent's risk "tolerance," the marginal rate of substitution between variance and expected return.

a. Derive the necessary equilibrium conditions for the stock market.

b. Demonstrate that domestic and foreign agents will, in general, not hold shares in the same world-market portfolio. Compare this result with exercise VI.13.2 where, under what is otherwise the same setup, taxation is based on the source principle.

---

1. This chapter also provides problems and solutions related to the material in chapter 12 of FR, "Capital Income Taxation in the Open Economy."

c. As a special case, suppose that the domestic tax factor is a constant fraction of the foreign tax factor: $(1 - t_h) = \gamma(1 - t_f)$, where $\gamma > 0$ and t_i $(i = h, f)$ denotes the tax rate for the domestic or foreign resident. Also assume that the riskless after-tax return differs by the same factor, γ, across countries. Show that under these conditions domestic and foreign agents will hold shares in the same world-market portfolio.

Solution

a. The exercise tries to provide further insights into the effects of government taxation in the open economy. With the focus on world stock markets and the riskiness of some assets, the analysis expands the arbitrage conditions of chapter 9 in FR which abstracted from uncertainty. These issues are further developed in chapter 13 of FR (see also exercises VI.13.1–VI.13.3).

The representative agent's budget constraint implies that initial wealth is allocated among the three assets:

$$x_{0j} + x_{1j} + x_{2j} = 1, \quad j = h, f. \tag{2}$$

In equation (2), x_{ij} indicates the share of initial wealth invested by the home (h) or foreign (f) country's consumer in each of the three assets; for example, x_{0h} denotes the proportion of initial wealth W_h that the home country invests in the riskless asset. The state-dependent portfolio return after taxes and per unit of wealth is therefore

$$V_j = x_{0j}R + (1 - t_j)x_{1j}R_1 + (1 - t_j)x_{2j}R_2$$
$$\equiv x_{0j}R + x_{1j}R_{1t}^j + x_{2j}R_{2t}^j, \quad j = h, f. \tag{3}$$

In equation (3), R_{it}^j denotes the after-tax return of asset i in country j. It differs across investors in the two countries since the tax rates, t_j, are based on the residence principles. Pretax returns are denoted by R_i. Domestic and foreign agents have common beliefs about the stochastic processes and are not subject to any short-sale restrictions. Solving the objective function (1) for optimal portfolio shares subject to the budget constraint (2) yields the following necessary conditions:

$$E\{R_{1t}^j\} - \frac{1}{\tau_j}(x_{1j}\sigma_1^2(t_j) + x_{2j}\sigma_{12}(t_j)) = \lambda_j \tag{4}$$

$$E\{R_{2t}^j\} - \frac{1}{\tau_j}(x_{2j}\sigma_2^2(t_j) + x_{1j}\sigma_{12}(t_j)) = \lambda_j \quad j = h, f \tag{5}$$

$$R = \lambda_j, \tag{6}$$

where $\sigma_{ik}(t_j)$ denotes the after-tax covariance of assets i and k. Note that asset returns and variances depend on a country's tax rate and are in general not the same in the two countries. Equations (4) and (5) describe the first-order condition for the optimal demand in domestic and foreign equity, respectively. Equation (6) indicates that the return on the riskless asset equals in equilibrium the marginal utility of wealth for both the domestic and the foreign consumer.

b. In this section it is to be shown that foreign and domestic agents will in general not hold the same portfolio of risky assets, the world-market portfolio. A necessary and sufficient condition for residents to hold the same portfolio is that the relative share of the two risky assets is identical in the portfolio held in each country. Combining equations (4) and (5) and substituting from equation (6) for the marginal utility of wealth yields the relative asset shares of domestic and foreign equities for the home and foreign countries:

$$\frac{x_{1h}}{x_{2h}} = \frac{1}{\frac{E\{R_{1t}^h\} - R}{E\{R_{2t}^h\} - R}\sigma_{12}(t_h) - \sigma_1^2(t_h)}\left(\sigma_{12}(t_h) - \frac{E\{R_{1t}^h\} - R}{E\{R_{2t}^h\} - R}\sigma_2^2(t_h)\right) \qquad (7a)$$

$$\frac{x_{1f}}{x_{2f}} = \frac{1}{\frac{E\{R_{1t}^f\} - R}{E\{R_{2t}^f\} - R}\sigma_{12}(t_f) - \sigma_1^2(t_f)}\left(\sigma_{12}(t_f) - \frac{E\{R_{1t}^f\} - R}{E\{R_{2t}^f\} - R}\sigma_2^2(t_f)\right). \qquad (7b)$$

Equation (7) illustrates that the portfolio shares in the home and foreign countries will generally be different since first and second moments of the after-tax equity returns are functions of a country's tax rate. This illustrates the proposition that tax rates based on the residence principle affect the efficient portfolio allocation across countries. On the other hand, after-tax returns and variances are identical for residents in both countries if taxation rules apply the source principle, as in the case discussed in exercise VI.13.2. With identical first and second moments of asset returns for agents in the two countries, it follows from a comparison of equations (7a) and (7b) that domestic and foreign agents will hold the same portfolio of risky assets. In the present model, taxation based on the source principle leads residents in both countries to hold the world-market portfolio.

c. Suppose that tax rates between the domestic and foreign countries differ by a factor γ where γ is a nonnegative constant. Consequently, after-tax returns and variances in the domestic and foreign country are linked according to

$$E\{R_{it}^h\} = \gamma E\{R_{it}^f\}, \quad \text{and} \quad R^h = \gamma R^f \tag{8}$$

with $i = 1, 2$.

$$\sigma_i^2(t_h) = \gamma^2 \sigma_i^2(t_f), \quad \text{and} \quad \sigma_{12}(t_h) = \gamma^2 \sigma_{12}(t_f) \tag{9}$$

Substituting equations (8) and (9) into the equilibrium conditions for portfolio shares described in equation (7) yields

$$\frac{x_{1h}}{x_{2h}} = \frac{x_{1f}}{x_{2f}}. \tag{10}$$

If taxes are proportional in the two countries, domestic and foreign agents will hold the same portfolio of risky assets, the world-market portfolio. While tax rates differ for domestic and foreign residents, the tax rate variations are nonstochastic and proportional. With linear preferences as in equation (1) such deviations do not affect the agent's allocation among risky assets.

Exercise V.9.2[2]

Consider a one-period model of a small open economy with two sectors and two consumption goods. Goods are internationally tradable and domestic production employs a constant returns-to-scale technology. The two inputs, labor and capital, are mobile across sectors but not across countries. Also assume that the economy is endowed with a fixed quantity of capital, K, while the quantity of labor input is part of the consumer's decision problem. There are six possible taxes available to the government: taxes on the two consumption goods, taxes on the two factors of production, and trade taxes on imports and exports. Suppose that the government selects taxes to maximize consumer welfare for a given government expenditure profile and subject to external constraints and the production possibility set.

a. Show that zero tax rates on trade are an optimum for the small open economy.

b. Derive the rules for optimal consumption taxes.

Solution

a. The first part of the exercise explores the optimal structure of trade taxes in a small open economy. To find the solution one can divide the decision

---

2. We are indebted to Eduardo Gonzalez for this problem and an earlier version of the solution.

problem into three parts, with the first two comprised of the producer and consumer decisions, and the third involving the optimal taxation problem faced by a benevolent government or social planner.

The *producer problem* is to choose labor inputs (L_i) and the distribution of capital (K_i) across sectors to maximize after-tax profits (π):

$$\pi = (1 - \tau_x)f^x(L_x, K_x) + (1 + \tau_m)pf^m(L_m, K_m)$$

$$- w(L_x + L_m) - r(K_x + K_m), \tag{1}$$

where τ_i denotes the tax rate on exportables and importables ($i = x, m$), p is the world-market price of importables with the world-market price for exportables as the numeraire, $f^i(\ )$ describes the constant returns-to-scale production functions, and w and r are the wage and interest rates, respectively. Firms are subject to constraints on capital ($K_x + K_m \leq K$) and labor inputs ($L_x + L_m \leq L$), where K denotes the capital endowment and L the total amount of labor supplied by households. Solving the producer's decision problem for the optimal allocation of labor yields

$$\frac{f_L^x}{f_L^m} = \frac{(1 + \tau_m)p}{(1 - \tau_x)}, \tag{2}$$

where f_L^i denotes the partial derivative of $f^i(\ )$ with respect to labor input in sector i.

The representative *consumer problem* is to maximize utility, defined over consumption of private and public goods and leisure, subject to the private-sector resource constraint:

$$\max_{\{c_x, c_m, L\}} U(c_x, c_m, 1 - L; G) \tag{3}$$

subject to:

$$(1 + \tau_{c_x})(1 - \tau_x)c_x + (1 + \tau_{c_m})(1 + \tau_m)c_m = (1 - \tau_w)wL + (1 - \tau_k)rK.$$

In equation (3), the maximum amount of labor is normalized to unity, and τ_{c_i} ($i = x, m$) denotes the consumption tax rates. Since labor taxes will not affect the subsequent results one can set $\tau_w = 0$ for the remainder of the problem. Capital is supplied inelastically so that taxes on capital are non-distortionary like lump-sum taxes. It is assumed that the desired level of government spending exceeds the potential proceeds from capital taxation. In this case, it is optimal to confiscate revenues derived from the existing capital stock so that $\tau_k = 1$. The solution to the consumer problem yields demand and labor-supply functions that depend on consumption and trade taxes as well as international prices and wages. Correspondingly, the private component of the indirect-utility function can be described by a function Γ: $\Gamma(\tau_{c_x}, \tau_{c_m}, \tau_x, \tau_m, p, w)$.

The benevolent *government's optimal taxation problem* is to choose taxes and the optimal allocation of labor and capital across sectors for a given level of government expenditure. Consistent with the producer and consumer problem, the social planner maximizes the private component of the consumer's indirect-utility function:

$$\max_{\{\tau_{c_i}, \tau_i, L_i, K_i\}} \Gamma(\tau_{c_x}, \tau_{c_m}, \tau_x, \tau_m, p, w) \qquad i = x, m \tag{4}$$

subject to:

$$c_x(\tau_{c_x}, \tau_{c_m}, \tau_x, \tau_m, p, w) + pc_m(\tau_{c_x}, \tau_{c_m}, \tau_x, \tau_m, p, w) + G$$

$$= f^x(L_x, K_x) + pf^m(L_m, K_m)$$

and $L_x + L_m \leq L$; $K_x + K_m \leq K$.

Solving the social planner's problem for the optimal allocation of labor across sectors implies that pretax marginal returns on labor are equalized with relative world-market prices:

$$\frac{f_L^x}{f_L^m} = p. \tag{5}$$

Comparing the social planner's allocation as described in equation (5) with the firms' labor demand in equation (2) yields the optimal rule for trade taxes:

$$\frac{1 + \tau_m}{1 - \tau_x} = 1. \tag{6}$$

According to equation (6) an optimum exists where trade taxes are zero: $\tau_x = \tau_m = 0$. Moreover, this is a necessary condition for an optimum if the possibility of trade subsidies is excluded ($\tau_i \geq 0, i = x, m$).[3] This is the familiar result from traditional trade theory models which state that optimal trade policy entails zero tariffs for the small open economy. Monopoly or, more generally, imperfect-competition arguments are necessary to justify trade taxes in this context.

---

3. If one allowed trade subsidies, equation (6) and the external constraint of a balanced trade account imply that net revenues from trade taxes would be zero. Revenues from import taxes would be just sufficient to cover the subsidy payments for exports, or vice versa.

b. To derive the conditions for optimal consumption taxes on importables and exportables, it is convenient to rewrite the private component of the indirect utility function. Using the results of part a, the function Γ can be reformulated in terms of after-tax prices and after-tax income (I): $\Gamma^*(p_x, p_m; I)$, where $p_x = 1 + \tau_{c_x}$ and $p_m = (1 + \tau_{c_m})p$. The Lagrangean function for the optimal consumption tax problem corresponding to equation (4), with the government's budget constraint explicitly incorporated, is

$$\mathscr{L} = \Gamma^*(p_x, p_m; I) + \lambda(G - (p_x - 1)c_x - (p_m - p)c_m - rK). \tag{7}$$

In equation (7), the term in brackets following the Lagrange multiplier (λ) captures the government's budget constraint: Total expenditures cannot exceed the sum of tax revenues from consumption taxes on importables and exportables and the expropriation of capital income. Solving the planner's problem yields the necessary condition for optimal consumption taxes:

$$\frac{\partial \Gamma^*}{\partial p_i} = \lambda \left\{ c_i + \tau_{c_x} \frac{\partial c_x}{\partial p_i} + \tau_{c_m} p \frac{\partial c_m}{\partial p_i} \right\}, \qquad i = x, m. \tag{8}$$

To derive the compensated demand functions one can use the derivative property of indirect-utility functions ($\partial \Gamma^*/\partial p_i = -c_i \mu$, where $\mu \equiv \partial \Gamma^*/\partial I$) and the Slutsky decomposition of the compensated demand elasticity (S_{ij}): $S_{ij} = \partial c_i/\partial I c_j + \partial c_i/\partial p_j$, $i = x, m$; $j = x, m$. Using these properties in equation (8) gives the necessary conditions for optimal consumption taxes in terms of the compensated price elasticities:

$$\tau_{c_x} S_{xx} + p\tau_{c_m} S_{mx} = \xi c_x \tag{9a}$$

$$\tau_{c_x} S_{xm} + p\tau_{c_m} S_{mm} = \xi c_m, \tag{9b}$$

where $\xi = \left\{ \tau_{c_x} \dfrac{\partial c_x}{\partial I} + \tau_{c_m} p \dfrac{\partial c_m}{\partial I} - \dfrac{\lambda + \mu}{\lambda} \right\}.$

Equation (9) can be solved for the optimal consumption tax rates τ_{c_i}. As a benchmark, consider the case where goods are unrelated in demand ($S_{ij} = 0$ for $i \neq j$). It follows from equation (9a) that $\tau_{c_x} = \xi/(S_{xx}/c_x)$. Recall that the compensated demand elasticity is defined as $\varepsilon_i \equiv S_{ii} p_i/c_i$. Substituting this expression for S_{xx}, one can rewrite equation (9a) for the benchmark case as

$$\tau_{c_x} = \frac{1}{\dfrac{\varepsilon_x}{\xi} - 1}. \tag{10}$$

This is an example of the familiar Ramsey taxation rules, and a corresponding formula applies to the consumption tax on importables. The optimal tax rate is (inversely) proportional to a good's demand elasticity. For example, consider the case where $\varepsilon_x \to -\infty$. As can be inferred from equation (10), the optimal tax rate becomes zero. If the demand for a good is highly elastic, even a small rise in the tax rate would lead to large substitution effects and thus a quick erosion of the tax base. As a general rule, it is optimal for tax rates to be higher on goods that have a relatively low demand elasticity.

Exercise V.9.3

Consider a small-country version of the overlapping generations model developed in chapter 7. Individuals have a constant probability of surviving each period (γ). Consumer preferences are homothetic over two consumption goods, and agents have constant relative risk aversion. Assume that the two consumption goods are internationally tradable and that the domestic country completely specializes in the production of exportables. The production technology for exportables is constant returns-to-scale and, assuming constant factor inputs, output remains fixed over time. Importables are subject to a proportional tariff whose revenues are distributed lump sum to living individuals. Finally, assume that the government follows a balanced-budget policy in all periods.

a. Describe the effects of a change in tariff rates on saving and the current account. Show that the qualitative response depends on a transfer criterion based on the domestic rate of time preference and the world rate of interest.

b. Discuss why tariffs have effects in this model even when one starts from a position of free trade, so that the distortion is of second order.

Solution

a. To assess the effects of a permanent change in tariff rates it will be convenient to use a continuous-time version of the overlapping generations model. The agent's preferences are defined over consumption of importables (c_1) and exportables (c_2). The certainty-equivalence form of preferences at time t_1 and for an agent born at time $s \le t_1$ is given by

$$\int_{t_1}^{\infty} U(c_1(s, t), c_2(s, t)) e^{-(\rho + \pi)(t - t_1)} \, dt, \tag{1}$$

where ρ denotes the pure rate of time preference and $\pi = 1 - \gamma \geq 0$ is the instantaneous death probability. At any time $t \geq s$ the agent's budget constraint is given by

$$\dot{m}(s, t) = (r + \pi)m(s, t) + i(s, t) - c_1(s, t) - p(t)c_2(s, t) + T(t). \tag{2}$$

The variable m denotes the sum of financial (b) and physical (k) capital holdings ($m = b + k$), the time derivative of a variable is indicated by a dot, and the variable i describes the agent's labor income. Foreign prices of consumption goods will be normalized to unity so that total consumption expenditure at foreign prices is given by $z = c_1 + c_2$. The domestic price of the importable good, p, depends on the prevailing tariff rate. With complete specialization in the production of exportables, per capita tariff revenues are given by $T(t) = (p(t) - 1)C_2(t)$, where capital letters denote aggregate per capita values of a variable. Tariff revenues are distributed lump sum and the government's budget is always balanced.

The production technology for exportable goods is constant returns-to-scale. Therefore, receipts from physical capital holdings are given by the excess of the value of production over labor costs:

$$rK(t) = Y_1(t) - I(t). \tag{3}$$

With complete specialization and constant labor supply, the values of capital and labor income are unchanged by variations in the tariff rate. Thus, $K(t)$ is a function of the rental rate of capital (r) alone, which is set constant in the small-country case.

Aggregating individual human wealth, that is, the sum of labor income and net transfers from the government, across cohorts yields per capita human wealth (H):

$$H(t_1) = \frac{1}{r + \pi}I + \int_{t_1}^{\infty} T(t)e^{-(\rho+\pi)(t-t_1)}\,dt, \tag{4}$$

where we used the result that labor income (I) is constant over time and identical across cohorts. With homothetic preferences and constant relative risk aversion, aggregate per capita consumption is proportional to aggregate wealth:

$$C(t) = (1 - s)[M(t) + H(t)]. \tag{5}$$

In the small-country case, the savings rate (s) is constant and $(1 - s) = r + \pi + (\rho - r)/\sigma$, where σ denotes the coefficient of relative risk aversion. Per capita consumption expenditure, $C(t)$, is divided between the consumption of importable and exportable goods. The division is governed by the real exchange rate and depends accordingly on the tariff rate:

$$C_1(t) = [1 - \eta(p)]C(t), \quad \text{and} \quad C_2(t) = \eta(p)C(t), \tag{6}$$

with the weight η bounded by zero and one: $0 \leq \eta \leq 1$.

To assess the effect of a change in tariffs we shall describe the dynamics of the economy in terms of two equations that capture the evolution of its external assets and consumption, respectively. In deriving these equations one can use the laws of motion that govern the evolution of capital assets (M) and human capital (H):

$$\dot{M}(t) = rM(t) + I + T(t) - C(t) \tag{7}$$

$$\dot{H}(t) = (r + \pi)H(t) - I - T(t). \tag{8}$$

The equations display the familiar result that the discount rate governing the accumulation of capital assets is different from the rate governing the accumulation of human wealth. In the case of human wealth, the effective discount rate depends not only on the market rate of interest but also on the agents' survival probability. As long as $\gamma < 1$, that is, $\pi > 0$, the effective interest rate on human capital will exceed the rate applicable to capital assets. Since the physical capital stock is constant, the change in total capital assets is identical to the change in the net foreign asset position:

$$\dot{M}(t) = \dot{B}(t). \tag{9}$$

Next define a parameter α by $\alpha(p) = [1 - (1/p)]\eta(p)$. Tariff revenues can be expressed as $T(t) = \alpha C(t)$ and expenditures in foreign currency units by $Z(t) = (1 - \alpha)C(t)$. Using these substitutions and combining equations (3), (7), and (9) yields the law of motion for net foreign-asset accumulation:

$$\dot{B}(t) = rB(t) + Y_1 - Z(t). \tag{10}$$

Equation (10) describes the balance-of-payments equilibrium. It is exclusively determined by private-sector transactions since we assume that the government runs a balanced budget in all periods and redistributes tariff receipts to domestic residents. According to equation (10) the accumulation of net foreign assets in the domestic economy is equal to the sum of net receipts on services, $rB(t)$, and the country's trade balance, $Y_1 - Z(t)$. Note that the schedule where net foreign-asset accumulation is zero ($\dot{B}(t) = 0$) is upward-sloping in the $B - Z$ plane.

Finally, using $Z(t) = (1 - \alpha)C(t)$ and combining equations (5) to (8) gives the law of motion for domestic consumption expenditure at world prices:

$$\dot{Z}(t) = [r + \pi - (1 - s)]Z(t) - (1 - \alpha)(1 - s)\pi[K + B(t)]. \tag{11}$$

It follows from equation (11) that a graph where consumption expenditure remains unchanged ($\dot{Z}(t) = 0$) can slope upward or downward in the $B - Z$ plane (the graphs are not shown here but the interested reader can easily draw them to illustrate the following discussion). If $(\rho - r) < 0$, the schedule is upward-sloping, and vice versa. If the schedule is upward-sloping, stability requires that its slope be steeper than the slope of the $\dot{B}(t) = 0$ schedule.

Equations (10) and (11) describe the dynamic system of the economy in terms of the variables B and Z. In a steady state these variables are stationary, and we find the steady-state values of net foreign assets (B^s) and consumption expenditures (Z^s) by setting the time derivatives in equations (10) and (11) equal to zero. Accordingly,

$$B^s = \frac{1}{r}(Z^s - Y_1). \tag{12}$$

Using equations (3) and (12), the steady-state value for consumption demand in terms of foreign prices is

$$Z^s = \frac{(1 - s)(1 - \alpha)\pi}{(1 - s)(r + (1 - \alpha)\pi) - r(r + \pi)}I. \tag{13}$$

The following discussion assumes that tariff revenues are increasing in the tariff rate for a given level of aggregate consumption outlays so that $\partial\alpha/\partial p > 0$. It can be shown that if the system is stable then the denominator in equation (13) is positive and therefore $Z^s > 0$. Using equations (10) and (12) and assuming saddle stability, the accumulation of net foreign assets can be described by

$$\dot{B}(t) = \lambda[B(t) - B^s], \tag{14}$$

where λ denotes the stable root of the system ($\lambda < 0$).

Suppose the economy is initially in a steady state and that the domestic government introduces an unanticipated permanent increase in the import tariff rate. Since the country's claims on foreigners are initially given, it follows from equation (14) that the instantaneous adjustments in net foreign assets are confined to changes that are proportional to the shift in the steady-state value:

$$\frac{d\dot{B}(t)}{dp} = -\lambda\frac{dB^s}{dp}. \tag{15}$$

In the following it will be convenient to express the tariff change in terms of α. This will entail no loss in generality with respect to the qualitative results since we assume $\partial\alpha/\partial p > 0$. Differentiating equation (13) and using the definition of the savings rate gives the effect of a change in the tariff rate on steady-state consumption expenditure:

$$\frac{dZ^s}{d\alpha} = \frac{(1-s)r\pi}{\sigma[(1-s)(r+(1-\alpha)\pi)-r(r+\pi)]^2}(r-\rho)I. \tag{16}$$

In the steady state, consumption expenditure in terms of foreign currency will increase or decrease in response to the rise in tariffs, depending on whether the interest rate exceeds or falls short of the pure rate of time preference. Moreover, the immediate adjustment in consumption expenditure $Z(t)$ will be in the opposite direction from the long-run adjustment. This can be seen by combining equation (15) with the differentiated equations (10) and (12) and recalling that the stable root λ is negative:

$$\frac{dZ}{d\alpha} = \frac{\lambda}{r}\frac{dZ^s}{d\alpha}. \tag{17}$$

Using these results and differentiating equation (10), the effect on the current account is exactly the dual of the change in consumption measured in foreign currency: $d\dot{B}(t)/d\alpha = -dZ(t)/d\alpha$. Accordingly, the response of the current account is a function of the differential between interest and time-preference rate:

$$\text{sign}\left\{\frac{d\dot{B}(t)}{d\alpha}\right\} = \text{sign}\{r-\rho\}. \tag{18}$$

Equation (18) demonstrates that the current account effect of a change in tariffs will depend on a transfer criterion, the relative magnitude of the interest rate and the consumer's instantaneous rate of time preference. An increase in tariffs will improve the current account position of the domestic economy if the interest rate exceeds the rate of time preference, and vice versa. In contrast to consumption expenditures, it follows from equation (15) that the adjustment in the current account to a change in the tariff rate is unidirectional. If the current account improves immediately following the imposition in the tariff then it will also improve in the new steady state, and the current account will deteriorate in the steady state if and only if it deteriorates immediately after the increase in the tariff rate.

b. The economic interpretation of the effect of a tariff on the economy's equilibrium hinges on the distributional implications of tariffs across generations. If planning horizons were infinite ($\gamma = 1$ and, alternatively, $\pi = 0$), then agents benefitting from the tariff in terms of redistributed income would be identical to those paying the tariff. Consequently, small tariff changes around an initially undistorted equilibrium would have no effects on expenditure in the present model (compare equation 16 for $\pi = 0$). But if the agent's planning horizon is finite then tariffs will have first-order wealth effects as long as the pure rate of time preference does not equal the world rate of interest. These distributional effects across generations lead to changes in the current account of a country even if the initial equilibrium is undistorted. To illustrate the argument, consider the case where $r > \rho$. At an arbitrary time, t, currently living agents will tend to accumulate capital assets. Consequently, they will have larger capital-asset holdings in future periods than agents who arrive in the economy only after time t. Since noncapital incomes are identical for all cohorts, this implies that agents currently alive will have a larger total wealth position in later periods than agents who enter the economy only after time t. The agent's wealth determines his expenditures since, under our assumptions regarding preferences, total spending is proportional to a consumer's wealth with the marginal propensity to consume $(1 - s)$ identical across agents of different cohorts. Consequently, agents alive at time t will consume more in absolute amounts in future periods than agents born in later periods if $r > \rho$. With proportional tariff rates, agents currently alive will thus also pay a larger amount of the tariff revenues. On the other hand, tariff receipts are distributed lump sum and equally to all agents. As a result, the wealth position of agents currently alive deteriorates vis-à-vis those who will be born in later periods. Domestic demand declines in the current period and the current account improves. Similar arguments apply if $r < \rho$. In future periods, the wealth of later generations will exceed the wealth of agents currently alive. With lump-sum redistribution of tariff revenues, an increase in the tariff rate will redistribute wealth away from future generations and improve the wealth position of present generations. This results in higher consumption and lower savings, and the current account deteriorates.

10

Budget Deficits with Distortionary Taxes

Exercise V.10.1

Consider the open-economy model with distortionary taxes presented in chapter 10. Assume that the path of government expenditure remains unchanged by modifications of the tax regime. Describe the effects of a budget deficit arising from the combined changes in the rates of taxation on labor and capital income.

a. What are the effects of a reduction in labor-income tax rates today accompanied by an offsetting change in future capital-income taxes?

b. What are the effects of a reduction in capital-income tax rates today accompanied by an offsetting change in future labor-income taxes?

Solution

a. In this problem we are asked to assess the effects of budget deficits that result from a combination of labor- and capital-income taxes. We begin by specifying the budget constraints for the private and public sectors and the economy's production technology.

The basic framework is the one-good, two-period model described in chapter 10 of Frenkel and Razin. Let the total amount of time available to a consumer be normalized to unity so that $(1 - n(t))$ indicates the consumer's time spent on nonmarket activities. Using full income to evaluate the household's wealth (W), its lifetime budget constraint is

$$C(0) + \frac{1}{R(0)} C(1) + [1 - \tau_1(0)][1 - n(0)]w(0)$$

$$+ \frac{1}{R(0)} [1 - \tau_1(1)][1 - n(1)]w(1)$$

$$= [1 - \tau_1(0)]w(0) + \frac{1}{R(0)}[1 - \tau_1(1)]w(1)$$

$$+ [1 - \tau_k(0)]r_k(0)K(0) + \frac{1}{R(0)}[1 - \tau_k(1)]r_k(1)K(0)$$

$$+ [1 - \tau_k(0)][\alpha_I r_k(1)K(I(0)) - I(0)] - R(-1)B^p(-1)$$

$$\equiv W(0), \tag{1}$$

where τ_1 and τ_k denote the marginal tax rates on labor and capital income, respectively. $C(t)$ indicates consumption in period $t = 0$, 1, $K(0)$ is the initial endowment of capital, and $w(t)$ and $r_k(t)$ denote the wage rate and the rental rate of capital, respectively. The effective discount factor for investment in physical capital, α_I, depends on the capital-income tax rates in the two periods as well as on the rate of return on financial assets (R): $\alpha_I = [1 - \tau_k(1)]/\{[1 - \tau_k(0)]R(0)\}$. For simplicity it is assumed that the capital stock does not depreciate and that the production technology is linear:

$$Y(0) = a(0)n(0) + b(0)K(0) \tag{2}$$

$$Y(1) = a(1)n(1) + b(1)[K(0) + K(I(0))]. \tag{3}$$

In equilibrium the marginal cost of labor and capital must be equal to their marginal returns: $a(t) = w(t)$, and $b(t) = r_k(t)$, for $t = 0$, 1. Moreover, optimal investment requires that returns on financial and physical investments are equalized:

$$R(0) = \frac{1 - \tau_k(1)}{1 - \tau_k(0)} r_k(1)K'(I(0)). \tag{4}$$

The government's intertemporal budget constraint requires that receipts from capital- and labor-income taxes are sufficient to service the initial government debt ($B^g(-1)$) and finance government expenditure (G) in the two periods:

$$G(0) + \frac{1}{R(0)}G(1) = \tau_1(0)w(0) + \frac{1}{R(0)}\tau_1(1)w(1) - R(-1)B^g(-1)$$

$$+ \tau_k(0)[\tau_k(0)K(0) - I(0)]$$

$$+ \frac{1}{R(0)}\tau_k(1)r_k(1)[K(0) + K(I(0))]. \tag{5}$$

Combining the government budget constraint in equation (5) with the household budget constraint in equation (1) and using the production functions in equations (2) and (3) yields the economywide budget constraint:

$$C(0) + \frac{1}{R(0)} C(1) = [a(0)n(0) + b(0)K(0) - G(0) - I(0)]$$

$$+ \frac{1}{R(0)} [a(1)n(1) + b(1)[K(0) + K(I(0))] - G(1)]$$

$$- R(-1)B(-1)$$

$$\equiv V(0). \tag{6}$$

In equation (6) the present value of the domestic economy's resources are denoted by $V(0)$. A similar equation describes the foreign country's resource constraint assuming that the production structure abroad is also linear. It will also be assumed that the foreign tax profile is flat so that it does not introduce intertemporal distortions, and that the foreign government runs a balanced budget in each period.

Consumer preferences are described by homothetic utility functions that are separable in consumption and leisure. Under these assumptions the only variables that would affect private consumption demand are the interest rate in period 0 and private-sector wealth: $C = C(R(0), W(0))$, and $C^* = C^*(R(0), W^*(0))$. Moreover, relative consumption demand in the two periods $(D = C(0)/C(1))$ is a nonincreasing function in the interest rate. Assuming that relative demand in at least one of the two countries is strictly decreasing in $R(0)$, the same will also hold for the relative world demand between the two periods, a weighted average of domestic and foreign relative intertemporal demand (see figure 10.1).

The intertemporal net supply of the domestic economy is defined as $z = [Y(0) - I(0) - G(0)]/[Y(1) - G(1)]$, and a corresponding definition applies to foreign intertemporal net supply. Since investment $(I(0))$ is decreasing in $R(0)$, a rise in $R(0)$ would be accompanied by rise in z on account of the investment response. At the same time, a change in the interest rate will also affect the agent's leisure choice through substitution and wealth effects. First, as $R(0)$ increases, the intertemporal substitution effect would increase the current-period opportunity costs for leisure and thereby lead to a higher labor input in the current period. Second, a rise in the interest rate would lower the agent's wealth as defined in equation (1) by decreasing the discounted value of future-period incomes. As long as leisure is a normal good this would increase labor input in both periods,

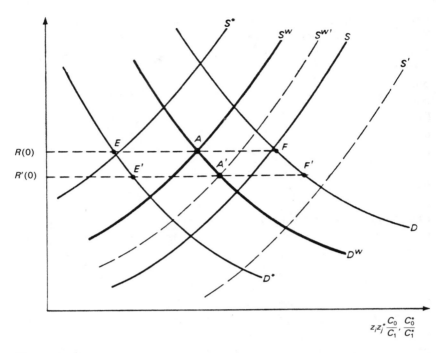

Figure 10.1
The effects of a budget deficit arising from changes in capital- and labor-income taxes

leaving the ensuing relative increase in output in the two periods ambiguous. It is assumed below that the wealth effect, if it counteracts the intertemporal substitution effect, would not dominate so that the intertemporal supply curve is an increasing function of the period 1 interest rate. This holds for the domestic (S) as well as for the foreign (S^*) supply functions and thereby also for the world intertemporal supply function (S^w), a weighted average of domestic and foreign supplies (see figure 10.1).

The previous derivations provide the framework to assess the effects of a current-period cut in labor-income taxes followed by a future rise in the capital-income tax rate that restores budgetary equilibrium. The increase in the future capital-income tax rate decreases ceteris paribus the effective discount factor for investment (α_I). At a given level of the financial interest rate ($R(0)$), investment demand would decline and the domestic intertemporal supply curve S would shift to the right. The cut in today's labor taxes would tend to increase the opportunity cost of leisure in the current period. Assuming that labor supply is not a Giffen good, so that labor inputs are increasing in after-tax compensation, the tax cut would increase current-period output. It is also assumed that any possible wealth effect (see below) could not reverse the relative output effect so that the decline in current-period labor taxes will increase current-period output relative to output in period 1. This reinforces the effect of the future capital-tax increase and the domestic intertemporal supply curve shifts to the right to S' (see figure 10.1). The shift in the domestic supply schedule leads to an outward shift in the world supply schedule. The latter shift is smaller and reflects the domestic economy's weight in the net world supply of goods in period 1. Since there is no direct effect on the domestic or foreign demand schedules, the interest rate will have to fall. In the new equilibrium depicted by point A' in figure 10.1, the decline in the interest rate from $R(0)$ to $R'(0)$ will result in a fall of demand growth in both the domestic and the foreign countries.

The equilibrium response of domestic investment and consumption levels in period 0 is ambiguous. With respect to investment, the increase in the future tax burden tends to lower investment activity. At the same time, part of the decline in the interest rate $R(0)$ is also induced by the cut in current-period labor taxes. If this effect outweighs the future tax effect so that the effective interest rate declines, then domestic investment could increase despite the increased burden on capital income. The ambiguity of the effect on consumption reflects possibly conflicting intertemporal substitution and wealth effects. Intertemporal substitution leads to higher consumption in period 0 as the interest rate declines. But the private wealth effect is ambiguous, which is partly because of the effects on wealth of the interest-rate-related changes in labor inputs. In addition, declining interest rates have a positive direct effect on wealth if the initial equilibrium is undistorted (compare equation 1). The wealth effect thus reinforces, the intertemporal substitution effect and domestic consumption in period 0 increases. On the other hand, if tax profiles are not flat initially, the complete wealth effect also depends on the degree of the initial distortions and is, in general, ambiguous. If the intertemporal substitution effect is relatively weak, a decline in wealth could dominate and domestic consumption levels in period 0 could decline.

Foreign investment activity rises in response to the decline in the interest rate. The declining interest rate also increases current-period consumption abroad on account of intertemporal substitution effects. Moreover, if the foreign equilibrium is undistorted initially the decline in interest rates will have a positive wealth effect as the discounted value of future incomes increases; compare the definition of $W^*(0)$, the foreign analogue of domestic private-sector wealth defined in equation (1). Both wealth and substitution effects result in an increase in foreign consumption in period 0 (ruling out a backward-bending saving function). With initially flat tax profiles in both countries, the budget deficit would thus crowd in foreign and domestic consumption in period 0 and lead to a positive correlation between consumption levels in the two countries. The foreign consumption increase augments the rise in foreign investment demand and aggregate foreign demand increases. At the same time, foreign output in period 0 would tend to decrease: Both the intertemporal substitution effect and the interest-rate-induced rise in wealth would lower labor input and thereby decrease output. With rising foreign demand and declining foreign output the trade balance of the foreign country would deteriorate in the current period and, conversely, the domestic country's trade balance improves.

b. The effects of a budget deficit arising from a current-period cut in capital-income taxes and a future rise in labor-income taxes are similar to those discussed in the previous section. The cut in the capital-income tax rate $\tau_k(0)$ reduces the tax rebate that investors receive for investments in physical capital (compare equation 1). The decline in the investment rebate lowers the effective discount factor for investment α_I and, at the initial return $R(0)$ on financial assets, investments in physical capital become less attractive. Consequently, investment $I(0)$ in the domestic country would decline for a given interest rate, and the domestic intertemporal supply schedule would tend to shift outward on account of the fall in today's capital-income tax. The increase in future labor-income taxes would reduce labor input in period 1 if labor is not a Giffen good. Thus, and also under assumptions similar to those made in the previous section, the rise in future labor taxes will reduce future output levels relative to the current period. This reinforces the effect from the cut in current-period capital taxes, and the domestic intertemporal supply schedule shifts outward to S' in figure 10.1. In line with the weight of the domestic economy, the world supply schedule would shift to the right as well from S^w to $S^{w'}$. On the other hand, the demand schedules would remain unchanged since preferences are homothetic and separable between consumption and leisure. In the new equilibrium, the interest rate will decline and domestic, foreign, and world consumption growth will all be lower than in the original equilibrium.

The qualitative effects of the budget deficit on intertemporal growth rates are thus similar to those arising from a current-period cut in labor taxes combined with a future rise in capital-income taxes. The same applies to the effects on current-period consumption and investment levels; the reader is referred to the previous section for a more detailed analysis.

Exercise V.10.2

Consider a small open-economy version of the overlapping generations model in chapter 7. Assume that individuals have a constant probability to survive each period (γ) and that their preferences can be described by a logarithmic expected-utility function. Government spending is financed by a consumption tax with proportional tax rates. Describe the effects of a budget deficit arising from a current cut in taxes. To maintain the government's solvency condition and original pattern of government purchases, assume that the current-period tax cut is offset by a corresponding rise in future taxes.

Solution

The exercise extends the discussion of deficits and distortionary taxes to the finite horizon model developed in chapter 7 of Frenkel and Razin. The basic consumer problem is identical to the one discussed in the chapter except for the introduction of distortionary consumption taxes. Suppose the consumer maximizes a logarithmic expected-utility function; with constant period-survival probability ($\gamma \leq 1$) as the only source of uncertainty, the certainty-equivalence form of the preference function at time t for a consumer born in period s is

$$\sum_{j=0}^{\infty} (\gamma\delta)^j \ln\{c(s, t + j)\} \qquad \text{for } s \leq t \tag{1}$$

where δ denotes the subjective discount factor ($0 < \delta < 1$) and $c(s, t)$ is consumption in period t of an agent born at time s ($s \leq t$). The consumer problem is to maximize the preference function as described in equation (1) subject to a sequence of one-period budget constraints:

$$[1 + \tau(t)]c(s, t) + b^p(s, t) = \frac{R(t - 1)}{\gamma} b^p(s, t - 1) + y(s, t) \quad \text{for } s \leq t. \tag{2}$$

The world-market price of the single consumption good is normalized to unity. With τ denoting the marginal consumption tax rate, the domestic price for consumers is $(1 + \tau)$. Consolidating the one-period budget constraints and imposing the solvency condition yields the intertemporal budget constraint for an agent born at time $s \leq t$:

$$\sum_{j=0}^{\infty} \gamma^j \alpha_j [1 + \tau(t + j)] c(s, t + j) = \frac{R(t - 1)}{\gamma} b^p(s, t - 1) + \sum_{j=0}^{\infty} \gamma^j \alpha_j y(s, t + j)$$

$$\equiv w^p(s, t), \tag{3}$$

where the discount factor is defined as $\alpha_j = 1/[R(t)R(t + 1) \ldots R(t + j - 1)]$, $\alpha_0 \equiv 1$, and $R(t + j)$ denotes the interest factor in period $t + j$. Furthermore, private wealth in period t of a consumer born at time s, $w^p(s, t)$, is defined as the sum of financial and human wealth. With nonzero marginal taxes, the effective discount rate regarding consumption purchases incorporates the tax rate as well as, in the standard way, the interest rate adjusted by the probability of survival: $\gamma^j \alpha_j [1 + \tau(t + j)]$.

Solving the consumer's problem yields the necessary conditions for optimal consumption choice:

$$(\gamma \delta)^j \frac{1}{c(s, t + j)} = \lambda \gamma^j \alpha_j [1 + \tau(t + j)] \qquad \text{for all } j \geq 0, s \leq t, \tag{4}$$

where λ denotes the shadow value associated with the budget constraint. Combining equation (4) with the definition of private wealth in equation (3) yields private consumption as a proportional function of private wealth, with the factor of proportionality depending on the marginal tax rate:

$$c(s, t) = \frac{(1 - \gamma \delta)}{1 + \tau(t)} w^p(s, t) \qquad \text{for } s \leq t. \tag{5}$$

It follows that after-tax consumption expenditures are independent of the marginal tax rate for given levels of private wealth.

Private wealth consists of human wealth, $h(t)$, defined as the present value of future labor-income streams, and the initial value of financial assets, $R(t - 1)/\gamma b^p(s, t - 1)$. With taxes levied only on consumption, aggregation of the different components of wealth across cohorts is identical to the nondistortionary tax case discussed in Frenkel and Razin. Accordingly, per capita private wealth is

$$W^p(t) = R(t - 1)B^p(t - 1) + H(t), \tag{6}$$

where capital letters denote per capita aggregates. With the consumption function being the same for agents of all cohorts, we can aggregate the function as specified in equation (5):

$$C(t) = \frac{(1 - \gamma\delta)}{1 + \tau(t)} W^p(t). \tag{7}$$

Per capita consumption is proportional to per capita private wealth, the sum of human and financial wealth, and the factor of proportionality depends on the consumption tax rate. Thereby, after-tax expenditures are a constant fraction of private wealth and ceteris paribus independent of the consumption tax.

Alternative time profiles of government taxes must satisfy the government's budget constraint. At time t, and assuming that the government's intertemporal solvency condition is satisfied, the per capita intertemporal budget constraint of the government is

$$\sum_{j=0}^{\infty} \alpha_j G(t + j) = R(t - 1)B^g(t - 1) + \sum_{j=0}^{\infty} \alpha_j T(t + j)$$

$$= R(t - 1)B^g(t - 1) + \sum_{j=0}^{\infty} \alpha_j \tau(t + j)C(t + j), \tag{8}$$

where G, B^g, and T denote per capita government spending, assets, and taxes, respectively. The last part of the equation reflects that consumption taxes are the only form of tax revenues for the government in the model.

Suppose the government institutes an unanticipated tax cut in period 0 followed by a uniform tax increase in all future periods that maintains solvency. From equation (6) it is evident that the tax cut leaves per capita wealth unchanged in period 0. The only effect on consumption is thus through the price effect associated with the decline in period 0 taxes. Differentiating equation (7), a tax cut in period 0 lowers period 0 consumption according to

$$\frac{dC(0)}{d\tau(0)} = -\frac{(1 - \gamma\delta)}{[1 + \tau(0)]^2} W^p(0) \le 0. \tag{9}$$

In contrast to the case of lump-sum taxes, where government deficits affect consumption through wealth effects, unanticipated tax cuts of marginal consumption taxes work through price effects. And compared to the infinite planning horizon model ($\gamma = 1$), the marginal effect of a tax cut is larger here (since $1 - \gamma\delta \ge 1 - \delta$). The larger marginal effect on consumption reflects the higher marginal propensity to consume out of wealth, $[1 - \gamma\delta]/[1 + \tau(0)]$, if agents are faced with a nonunitary probability of survival. Combining the relatively large response to tax cuts and the larger propensity to consume if the planning horizon is finite, it is straightforward to show that the elasticity of consumption with respect to the tax cut is un-affected by the agent's planning horizon: $\varepsilon_{C(0),\tau(0)} = -\tau(0)/[1 + \tau(0)] \leq 1$. Moreover, the elasticity of consumption with respect to the current price $[1 + \tau(0)]$ is unity; see equation (7). After-tax expenditures are independent of the tax rate in the case of logarithmic preferences.

A tax cut in the current period is followed by uniform increases in the marginal tax rate in all future periods to maintain government solvency. As a benchmark, consider the case where tax rates are initially constant in all periods, the world rate of interest is constant with $R\delta = 1$, and there is no outstanding debt at the beginning of period 0. Under these assumptions, and if the stream of endowment incomes (y) is constant across time, per capita consumption will also be constant in all periods in the initial equilib-rium. From the government's budget constraint (8), a tax cut in period 0 would require future uniform tax increases according to

$$\frac{d\tau}{d\tau(0)} = -(R - 1). \tag{10}$$

Future tax hikes would result in a uniform decline in consumption in all future periods $dC(j) = dC(j + 1) \leq 0$ for $j \geq 1$. The decline reflects only the price effect, that is, the increase in future tax rates, as indicated by the consumption function (7). Since after-tax consumption expenditures, $[1 + \tau(0)]C(0)$, are invariant to the unanticipated tax cut, financial wealth remains constant over time. By assumption, human wealth is also constant, and per capita private wealth, the sum of human and financial wealth, remains therefore unchanged in the benchmark case by a temporary cut in marginal consumption tax rates. The effects of temporary unanticipated tax cuts work thus exclusively through price effects.

Exercise V.10.3

Consider a two-period model of a small open-endowment economy with one consumption good. Suppose the government chooses the distribution of consumption taxes over time to maximize consumer welfare for a given level of government expenditure. Also assume that the government has initially no domestic and foreign debt or assets and that government ex-penditures are constant across periods. Derive the conditions under which the optimal intertemporal tax policy would imply a budget deficit in the first period followed by a budget surplus in the second period.

Solution

The goal of this exercise is to find the optimal time profile for consumption taxes. As such, it complements in an intertemporal context exercise V.9.2 where the focus was on optimal temporal tax rules. Once we find here the intertemporal tax rates we also have the means to assess conditions for optimal budget deficits.

The consumer's decision problem is to maximize utility by choosing a consumption path $\{c_t\}$ for periods $t = 1, 2$. The world-market price of the nonstorable consumption good is normalized to unity and the small open economy faces a given interest rate in period 1, R_1. Assuming no initial private debt, the consumer solves

$$\max_{\{c_1, c_2\}} U(c_1, c_2; G) \tag{1}$$

subject to

$$(1 + \tau_{c_1})c_1 + \frac{1}{R_1}(1 + \tau_{c_2})c_2 = Y_1 + \frac{1}{R_1}Y_2,$$

where Y_t denotes the endowment and τ_{ct} the consumption tax rate in period t. Solving the problem in equation (1) for fixed government expenditure (G) gives the familiar necessary condition that the intertemporal marginal rate of substitution must be equal to the relative intertemporal after-tax price:

$$\frac{\partial U/\partial c_2}{\partial U/\partial c_1} = \frac{1}{R_1}\frac{(1 + \tau_{c_2})}{(1 + \tau_{c_1})}. \tag{2}$$

The solution to the consumer problem yields demand functions that depend on the after-tax prices and after-tax income (I): $c_i = c_i(p_1, p_2^*, I)$, $i = 1$, 2, where $p_1 = (1 + \tau_{c_1})$ and $p_2^* = (1 + \tau_{c_2})/R_1$. Note that p_2^* is the discounted future price of the consumption good; the intertemporal substitution effect depends on the interest rate as well as on the future price of consumption. Corresponding to the consumption demand functions one can write the indirect-utility function (V) as $V = V(p_1, p_2^*, I)$.

The government's optimal tax problem is to choose the profile of consumption taxes that will maximize private-sector welfare. Incorporating the government's budget constraint, the Lagrangean function for the government decision problem is

$$\mathcal{L} = V(p_1, p_2^*; I) + \lambda \left[G - (p_1 - 1)c_1 - \left(p_2^* - \frac{1}{R_1} \right)c_2 \right].$$ (3)

In equation (3), the term in square brackets following the Lagrange multiplier (λ) captures the government's budget constraint: Total expenditure cannot exceed the sum of tax revenues from consumption taxes in the two periods. Solving the planner's problem yields the necessary conditions for optimal consumption taxes:

$$\frac{\partial V}{\partial p_1} = \lambda \left\{ c_1 + \tau_{c_1} \frac{\partial c_1}{\partial p_1} + \tau_{c_2} \frac{1}{R_1} \frac{\partial c_2}{\partial p_1} \right\}$$ (4a)

$$\frac{\partial V}{\partial p_2^*} = \lambda \left\{ c_2 + \tau_{c_1} \frac{\partial c_1}{\partial p_2^*} + \tau_{c_2} \frac{1}{R_1} \frac{\partial c_2}{\partial p_2^*} \right\}.$$ (4b)

To derive the compensated demand functions one can use the derivative property of indirect-utility functions ($\partial V/\partial p_1 = -c_1 \mu$, $\partial V/\partial p_2^* = -c_2 \mu$, where $\mu \equiv \partial V/\partial I$) and the analogue of the Slutsky decomposition for the intertemporal case: $S_{ij} = \partial c_i/\partial Ic_j + \partial c_i/\partial p_j$, $i = 1, 2$; $j = 1, 2$. Using these properties in equation (4) gives the necessary conditions for optimal consumption taxes in terms of the compensated price elasticities:

$$\tau_{c_1} S_{11} + \frac{1}{R_1} \tau_{c_2} S_{21} = \psi c_1$$ (5a)

$$\tau_{c_1} S_{12} + \frac{1}{R_1} \tau_{c_2} S_{22} = \psi c_2,$$ (5b)

where $\psi = \left\{ \tau_{c_1} \frac{\partial c_1}{\partial I} + \tau_{c_2} \frac{1}{R_1} \frac{\partial c_2}{\partial I} - \frac{\lambda + \mu}{\lambda} \right\}.$

Equation (5) can be solved for the optimal consumption tax rates τ_{c_i}. Consider a benchmark case where goods are unrelated in demand ($S_{ij} = 0$ for $i \neq j$). It follows from equation (5a) that $\tau_{c_1} = \psi/(S_{11}/c_1)$. The compensated demand elasticity is defined as $\varepsilon_i \equiv S_{ii}p_i/c_i$, and substituting this expression for S_{11}, one can rewrite equation (5a) for the benchmark case as

$$\tau_{c_1} = \frac{1}{\dfrac{\varepsilon_1}{\psi} - 1}.$$ (6a)

Similar substitutions yield the corresponding rule for optimal consumption taxes in the second period:

$$\tau_{c_2} = \cfrac{1}{\cfrac{\varepsilon_2}{\psi} - 1}. \tag{6b}$$

These are examples of the familiar Ramsey taxation rules applied in the intertemporal context. If consumption demand were less elastic in a particular time period, then optimal tax rates would be comparatively high during this period. In general, though, there is not much evidence that price elasticities for aggregate demand functions show systematic variations over time. Suppose therefore that the compensated demand elasticities are the same in the two periods: $\varepsilon_1 = \varepsilon_2$. Under these conditions, optimal taxation requires constant tax rates over time in the benchmark case: $\tau_{c_1} = \tau_{c_2}$. Whether the government runs a deficit or surplus in the first period depends only on the relative consumption demand in the two periods:

$$\text{sign}\{g_1 - \tau_{c_1}c_1\} = -\text{sign}\{c_1 - c_2\}, \tag{7}$$

where g_1 denotes government spending in the first period and it is assumed that initial government debt is zero. Underlying the condition in equation (7) is the result that constant tax rates imply higher government revenues $(\tau_{ct}c_t)$ in a period where consumption levels are comparatively high. Since, by assumption, government spending is constant over time, the government would have a deficit in periods where private consumption, and thereby tax revenues, are relatively low. To illustrate the case, suppose that private-sector preferences can be represented by a standard separable utility function with δ denoting the subjective discount factor. It follows from equation (2) that consumption in period 1 falls short of consumption in period 2 if $\delta R_1 > 1$. If the rate of interest exceeds the subjective rate of time preference ($\rho = (1 - \delta)/\delta$), then relatively more would be consumed in the second period and the government would have a budget deficit in the first period and a corresponding surplus in the second period.

The results here demonstrate that Ramsey-type optimal tax rules require constant tax rates over time if preference parameters are stable. But constant tax rates do not imply a balanced budget. In general, a balanced budget does not constitute an optimal fiscal stance in this model.

11

Fiscal Policies and
the Real Exchange Rate

Exercise V.11.1

Consider a two-period model of a small country. Agents receive endowments of a tradable (Y_T) and a nontradable (Y_N) good in each period t $(t = 0, 1)$. Agents' preferences are given by

$$U = [C_0^{1-1/\sigma} + DC_1^{1-1/\sigma}]/(1 - 1/\sigma), \tag{1}$$

where $C_t = c_{Tt}^{1-b}c_{Nt}^b$; c_T and c_N denote consumption levels of tradable and nontradable goods; and D denotes the subjective discount factor. There is perfect capital mobility; agents can borrow or lend at the world interest rate r^*, measured in terms of tradable goods, the numeraire.

a. Suppose that agents receive, in period 0 only, an exogenous increase in their endowment of tradable goods, Y_{T0}. What will the impact of this increase be on: the real exchange rate in each period; the real (consumption-based) discount factor; the trade balance (both in terms of tradables and consumption-based); and welfare? In your answer, you may assume that trade is initially balanced and that there is no initial debt.

b. How would your answers change if agents had no access to the world capital market?

Solution

a. We first solve for the real spending functions by maximizing (1) subject to the constraint

$$P_0 C_0 + RP_1 C_1 = W, \tag{2}$$

where as usual P_t is the exact price index in period t, R is the world discount factor (equal to 1 divided by 1 plus the world interest rate r^*), and W is wealth. Solving the first-order conditions yields the following real spending functions:

$$C_0 = W/\{P_0[1 + (RP_1/P_0)^{1-\sigma}D^\sigma]\}, \tag{3a}$$

$$C_1 = W(RP_1/P_0)^{1-\sigma}D^\sigma/\{RP_1[1 + (RP_1/P_0)^{1-\sigma}D^\sigma]\}, \tag{3b}$$

and, since under Cobb-Douglas utility we know that expenditure shares are constant, we have that

$$c_{NO} = bW/\{p_0[1 + (RP_1/P_0)^{1-\sigma}D^\sigma]\}, \tag{4a}$$

$$c_{TO} = (1 - b)W/\{[1 + (RP_1/P_0)^{1-\sigma}D^\sigma]\}, \tag{4b}$$

$$c_{N1} = bW(RP_1/P_0)^{1-\sigma}D^\sigma/\{Rp_1[1 + (RP_1/P_0)^{1-\sigma}D^\sigma]\}, \tag{4c}$$

$$c_{T1} = (1 - b)W(RP_1/P_0)^{1-\sigma}D^\sigma/\{R[1 + (RP_1/P_0)^{1-\sigma}D^\sigma]\}, \tag{4d}$$

where the price index $P_t = kp_t^b$ with k a positive constant, and where p_t represents the relative price of nontradables or the reciprocal of the real exchange rate. The equilibrium conditions state that demand and supply for nontradable goods must be equal in each period:

$$c_{NO} = Y_{NO}, \tag{5a}$$

$$c_{N1} = Y_{N1}. \tag{5b}$$

Totally differentiating equations (5a) and (5b) and using the definition of wealth,

$$W = Y_{TO} + p_0 Y_{NO} + R(Y_{T1} + p_1 Y_{N1}), \tag{6}$$

enables one to solve for the effects on the real exchange rate in each period:

$$d\log p_0/d\log Y_{TO} = (1 - \gamma), \tag{7a}$$

$$d\log p_1/d\log Y_{TO} = (1 - \gamma), \tag{7b}$$

where $(1 - \gamma)$ denotes the ratio of the value of current spending to lifetime wealth. An increase in the endowment of tradable goods increases lifetime wealth and thereby increases spending on all goods in all periods. The increase in consumption of nontradables creates an incipient excess demand for this type of good, the elimination of which requires an appreciation of the real exchange rate in both periods. Notice that, although the increase in the endowment is confined to period 0, the real exchange rate is affected in both periods.

With constant expenditure shares and equiproportionate increases in the relative price of nontradables in both periods, the price indices P_0 and P_1 will also rise by the same proportion. Therefore, the increased endowment of tradable goods will have no effect on the consumption discount factor, RP_1/P_0. This result is intuitive. The excess supply of tradable goods engendered by the supply shock can simply be sold abroad via a surplus on the trade account. No change in the intertemporal profile of consumption is required, and hence no change in the intertemporal relative price is required, in order to ensure that equilibrium in this small country is continuously maintained. The change in the trade balance (measured either in terms of the consumption basket or in terms of the numeraire[1]) can be derived by differentiating the expression

$$TA_0 = Y_{T0} - c_{T0}, \tag{8}$$

to yield

$$dTA_0/dY_{T0} = \gamma. \tag{9}$$

Finally, differentiating (3a) and (3b) gives

$$dC_0/d\log Y_{T0} = (1 - b)(1 - \gamma)C_0 > 0, \tag{10a}$$

$$dC_1/d\log Y_{T0} = (1 - b)(1 - \gamma)C_1 > 0, \tag{10b}$$

and therefore

$$dU/d\log Y_{T0} = U_0\, dC_0/d\log Y_{T0} + U_1\, dC_1/d\log Y_{T0} > 0, \tag{11}$$

where U_0 and U_1 denote marginal utilities corresponding to period 0 and 1 consumption.

b. If there were no capital mobility, the trade account would need to be balanced in each period, and therefore consumption of each good would simply be equal to the endowment of each good in each period. The increase in the endowment of tradable goods in period 0 would not affect the real exchange rate in period 1 but would cause a real appreciation in period 0 because income in that period would have risen and a real appreciation would be necessary to choke off the incipient excess demand for nontradables. Welfare would still rise.

---

1. Recall the assumption that the trade account is initially balanced.

Exercise V.11.2

Consider an economy consisting of a representative consumer who derives utility in period t ($t = 1, 2$) by consuming N_t units of a nontraded good and M_t units of an imported consumption good. The utility function is

$$U(N_t, M_t) = [1/(1 - \theta)][N_t^\beta M_t^{(1-\beta)}]^{(1-\theta)}, \qquad \theta \geq 0, 0 < \beta < 1. \tag{1}$$

When $\theta = 1$, the utility function takes the logarithmic form. Letting the constant $\rho > 0$ denote the subjective rate of time preference, the consumer's welfare is given by

$$V = U(N_1, M_1) + [1/(1 + \rho)]U(N_2, M_2). \tag{2}$$

On the production side, resources are competitively allocated between the nontraded-goods sector and the export sector, where they produce N_t and X_t units of output, respectively. The economy's production possibilities are given by

$$X_t = f(N_t), \qquad f' < 0, f'' \leq 0. \tag{3}$$

We assume that X_t is not consumed domestically. All units of X_t are sold on world markets in exchange for M_t (which is not produced at home) or an internationally traded bond whose return is equal to r. We consider a small open economy that takes the world interest rate (r) and the terms of trade as given. For simplicity, we set the terms of trade to be equal to unity in both periods.

a. The representative consumer's objective is to maximize (2) subject to the intertemporal budget constraint:

$$f(N_1) + [1/(1 + r)]f(N_2) = M_1 + [1/(1 + r)]M_2. \tag{4}$$

Write down the first-order conditions for the consumer's problem. Show that if $\rho = r$, the agent consumes the same bundle in both periods.

b. Suppose now that an unanticipated binding quota is imposed in period 1, limiting imports of good M to $\overline{M}$, and scheduled to be lifted in period 2, returning the economy to a free trade position. Assume that the import license is granted to consumers free of charge and also that $\rho = r$. What are the first-order conditions for the consumer's problem in this case? Show that if $\theta = 1$, the quota generates an improvement in the trade balance in period 1 that is smaller than the reduction in imports. Show that, if θ is sufficiently large, the temporary quota will actually cause the current account in period 1 to deteriorate.

Solution

a. Apart from the budget constraint, the four first-order conditions are

$$U_{M_1}(N_1, M_1) = \lambda, \tag{5a}$$

$$U_{N_1}(N_1, M_1) = -\lambda f'(N_1), \tag{5b}$$

$$U_{M_2}(N_2, M_2) = \lambda(1 + \rho)/(1 + r), \quad \text{and} \tag{5c}$$

$$U_{N_2}(N_2, M_2) = -\lambda f'(N_2)(1 + \rho)/(1 + r), \tag{5d}$$

where λ denotes a Lagrange multiplier. Dividing (5a) by (5b) and (5c) by (5d) sets the marginal rate of substitution (MRS) equal to the marginal rate of transformation (MRT) between tradables and nontradables in each period[2]:

$$U_{M_t}(N_t, M_t)/U_{N_t}(N_t, M_t) = -1/f'(N_t) \equiv RER_t(N_t), \quad t = 1, 2, \tag{6}$$

where RER_t denotes the real exchange rate in period t (which by the transformation function only depends on the level of N_t). Furthermore, dividing (5a) by (5c) gives

$$U_{M_1}(N_1, M_1)/U_{M_2}(N_2, M_2) = (1 + r)/(1 + \rho). \tag{7}$$

From equation (7), it follows immediately that if $r = \rho$, $U_{M_1} = U_{M_2}$; that is, marginal utilities are equated across periods. From the properties of the transformation function, an increase in N_t reduces RER_t and thereby reduces the RHS of equation (6). Because preferences are homothetic, a reduction in the relative price of tradable goods (a fall in RER) reduces the optimal ratio of consumption of nontradables to tradables, N_t/M_t. Thus, along the optimal consumption path, rises in N_t, and hence falls in RER_t, will be associated with decreases in N_t/M_t.

Consider a situation in which $N_1 = N_2$. From (6), $RER_1 = RER_2$, and from the previous argument, $N_1/M_1 = N_2/M_2$. Must the level of imports be equal in the two periods? To answer this question, one need only note that with preferences as specified in (1), the marginal utility of imports U_{M_t} is a monotonic (decreasing) function of the level of imports, M_t. In order to satisfy equation (7) which requires that marginal utility be equated

---

2. Recall that, because there are no terms-of-trade shocks (the relative price between imports and exports is constant), there really is a Hicksian composite called tradable here. Moreover, we have chosen units such that the terms of trade are equal to unity. This means that the MRT between N and M is equal to the MRT between N and X, since the MRT between M and X (in trade) is equal to 1.

across the two periods, it follows immediately that $M_1 = M_2$, and therefore that the consumption bundles must be identical in the two periods.

b. With a binding quota, M_1 is no longer a choice variable. The problem of the consumer is therefore to choose consumption levels to maximize (2) subject to (4) and the additional constraint:

$$M_1 = \overline{M}. \tag{8}$$

Substituting (8) into (2) and (4) and maximizing the Lagrangean function with respect to the remaining three variables gives the following first-order conditions:

$$\beta(N_1^\beta \overline{M}^{(1-\beta)})^{(1-\theta)}/N_1 = \lambda/RER(N_1), \tag{9a}$$

$$\beta(N_2^\beta M_2^{(1-\beta)})^{(1-\theta)}/N_2 = \lambda[(1 + \rho)/(1 + r)]/RER(N_2), \tag{9b}$$

$$(1 - \beta)(N_2^\beta M_2^{(1-\beta)})^{(1-\theta)}/M_2 = \lambda[(1 + \rho)/(1 + r)], \tag{9c}$$

where, as before, λ is a Lagrange multiplier. Combining (9a) and (9b) gives

$$N_2/N_1[(N_1^\beta \overline{M}^{(1-\beta)})/(N_2^\beta M_2^{(1-\beta)})]^{(1-\theta)} = RER(N_2)/RER(N_1), \tag{10}$$

where we have imposed that $r = \rho$. Similarly, combining (9b) and (9c) gives

$$N_2/M_2 = [\beta/(1 - \beta)]RER(N_2). \tag{11}$$

Equations (4) (upon substitution of equation 8), (10), and (11) allow one to solve for the three endogenous variables, N_1, N_2, and M_2. Given knowledge of N_t, we can solve for $X_t = f(N_t)$ and for $RER_t = -1/f'(N_t)$.

Consider first the case where $\theta = 1$. In this case, equation (10) implies that $N_1 = N_2$, which in turn implies that $X_1 = X_2$ and $RER_1 = RER_2$. We next want to show that $N_1 = N_2 > N^*$ where N^* denotes the level of consumption of nontraded goods under free trade. Suppose this is not so; that is, suppose $N_1 = N_2 \leq N^*$. In the latter case, satisfaction of equation (11) requires $M_2 \leq M_2^*$ where M_2^* denotes the level of consumption of imports under free trade. But then equation (4) with $\overline{M} < M_1^*$ (where the latter denotes the free trade level of imports in period 1) cannot be satisfied since the righthand side will be strictly less than the lefthand side. We conclude therefore that $N_1 = N_2 > N^*$; that is, consumption of nontradables is higher with the quota than under free trade. It follows immediately that production of exports is lower under the quota than under free trade (equation 3). The conclusion is therefore that the trade balance improves by less than the reduction in imports imposed by the quota.

Consider now the case where θ is very large, and suppose for simplicity that θ tends to infinity or, put differently, that the intertemporal elasticity of substitution is very close to zero. In this case, the only way to satisfy equation (10) is for the flow of utility in each period to be equal. This result is intuitive since, when utilities in the two periods are very poor substitutes, small deviations from a flat utility path carry very high disutility costs. In the case where θ tends to infinity, the only way of avoiding these very large costs is by having a perfectly flat utility profile.

We next want to show that a flat utility profile implies that $N_1 > N_2$. Consider first the case in which $N_1 = N_2$. To equalize the flow of utility in the two periods, we must have $M_2 = \overline{M}$. To satisfy the budget constraint with equality, we must have $N_1 = N_2 > N^*$ where N^* is the consumption of home goods (in each period) under free trade (since $\overline{M} < M^*$ where M^* denotes the constant volume of imports under free trade). But then the lefthand side of equation (11) is higher than under free trade while the righthand side is lower, a contradiction. Therefore, $N_1 = N_2$ is not a possible equilibrium.

Consider the case in which $N_1 < N_2$. From equation (10), we know this is only compatible with a flat utility profile if $\overline{M} > M_2$. Since $\overline{M} < M^*$, we have immediately that $M_2 < M^*$ and therefore from (11) it must be the case that $N_2 < N^*$. But if $N_1 < N_2 < N^*$ and $M_2 < \overline{M} < M^*$, it is not possible for the budget constraint to be satisfied with equality. We conclude therefore that $N_1 > N_2$.

Moreover, it is straightforward to see that N_2 must be less than N^*, the constant level of nontradables consumption in the absence of the quota. The reason is that if $N_2 \geq N^*$, (11) would require that $M_2 \geq M^*$, which in turn would imply that the constant utility level is at least as large under the quota regime as under free trade, a contradiction.[3] We conclude therefore that $N_2 < N^*$ and therefore that $RER_2 > RER^*$ (where the latter is the constant real-exchange-rate level under free trade). From (11), it follows immediately that $M_2 < M^*$, and from the fact that $N_2 < N^*$, we know that $X_2 > X^*$. Since under free trade with $r = \rho$, $X^* = M^*$, we conclude that the country runs a trade surplus in period 2, and therefore, in order to satisfy its budget constraint with equality, a trade deficit is run in period 1.

The intuition of this result is straightforward. When the intertemporal elasticity of substitution is very low, agents choose a fairly flat utility

---

3. Note that if the allocation in the second period were identical with and without the quota, and the flow of utility were identical across periods, then equation (10) would not hold.

profile over time. The quota in period 1 lowers the flow of utility in period 1 relative to period 2. In order to achieve an absolutely flat utility profile, as is required when θ is infinite, the consumer must borrow in the first period; the counterpart is a trade deficit. Another way of stating this is that the desire to have a flat utility profile creates an incipient excess demand for nontradables in the first period relative to the second period. To eliminate this excess demand, the real exchange rate must appreciate in period 1 relative to period 2, which tends to crowd out first-period exports. It is this reduction in exports that generates the worsening in the trade balance despite the reduction in imports achieved by the quota.

Exercise V.11.3

Consider a two-period model of a small open economy. In each period, agents receive an endowment of a nontraded and an exportable good, where the latter is assumed not to be consumed domestically. Agents consume nontradables and importables, of which there is no domestic endowment. There is perfect capital mobility. Preferences are given by

$$U = [C_1^{1-1/\sigma} + DC_2^{1-1/\sigma}]/(1 - 1/\sigma), \tag{1}$$

where

$$C_t = [c_{nt}^{1-1/\varepsilon} + c_{mt}^{1-1/\varepsilon}]/(1 - 1/\varepsilon), \qquad t = 0, 1, \tag{2}$$

and where D is the subjective discount factor, and c_{nt} and c_{mt} denote, respectively, consumption of nontradables and imports in period t, $t = 0, 1$. The parameter σ denotes the intertemporal elasticity of substitution while the parameter ε denotes the intratemporal elasticity of substitution between nontradables and importables.

a. Find the effect on the consumption rate of interest of a temporary deterioration in the terms of trade. What role does the parameter ε play in your answer? How is the behavior of the real interest rate affected by the adjustment of the real exchange rate? In deriving your results, you may assume that the initial equilibrium is stationary in the sense that subjective and world discount factors are equal and expenditure shares are constant through time.

b. Does a deterioration in the terms of trade worsen or improve the (real) trade balance? What roles do the parameters ε and σ play in your answer? In your answer, you may assume that the trade account is initially balanced.

Solution

a. Solving for the real spending functions in the usual manner gives

$$C_1 = W/[P_1^\sigma(P_1^{1-\sigma} + DP_2^{1-\sigma})], \tag{3a}$$

$$C_2 = W/[P_2^\sigma(P_1^{1-\sigma} + DP_2^{1-\sigma})], \tag{4b}$$

where W (lifetime wealth) is given by

$$W = Y_{x1} + p_{n1}Y_{n1} + DY_{x2} + Dp_{n2}Y_{n2}, \tag{5}$$

where the subjective and world discount factors are assumed to be equal and where p_{nt} denotes the relative price of nontradables in period t, and Y_{it} denotes the endowment of good $i = x, n$ in period $t = 1, 2$. Solving now for the within-period demands gives

$$c_{nt} = P_t C_t / [(p_{mt}^{1-\varepsilon} + p_{nt}^{1-\varepsilon})p_{nt}^\varepsilon], \tag{6a}$$

$$c_{mt} = P_t C_t / [(p_{mt}^{1-\varepsilon} + p_{nt}^{1-\varepsilon})p_{mt}^\varepsilon], \tag{6b}$$

where c_{it} denotes the demand for good $i = n, m$ in period t and p_{mt} denotes the relative price of imports in period t (the terms of trade).

The consumption discount factor (which is equal to 1 over 1 plus the consumption interest rate) is given by

$$R_c = RP_2/P_1, \tag{7}$$

where R is the exogenous world discount factor which is assumed equal to D. Clearly, R_c depends on the price indices, P_2 and P_1, which in turn depend on the exogenous terms of trade p_{m1} and p_{m2} and the endogenous real exchange rates p_{n1} and p_{n2}. Differentiating equation (7) around an initial equilibrium with constant expenditure shares gives

$$d\log R_c/d\log p_{m1} = -b - (1-b)d\log q/d\log p_{m1}, \tag{8}$$

where $q = p_{n1}/p_{n2}$ denotes the intertemporal real-exchange-rate ratio, and b denotes the initial expenditure share of imports. A temporary deterioration in the terms of trade (a rise in p_{m1} with p_{m2} constant) directly increases the cost of current consumption relative to future consumption; that is, it increases the consumption rate of interest (lowers the consumption discount factor, R_c). This is captured by the first term in equation (8). The consumption discount factor also depends on the path of the real exchange rate, captured by the variable q. If q rises in response to the deterioration in the terms of trade, the movement in the real exchange rate contributes to a further rise in the consumption rate of interest, and conversely. To determine the effects on q of the movement in the terms of trade, it is necessary to differentiate the market-clearing conditions for nontradable goods to obtain

$$d \log q / d \log p_{m1} = b(\varepsilon - \sigma)/[b\varepsilon + (1 - b)\sigma]. \tag{9}$$

The intuition of this expression is as follows. A rise in p_{m1} causes consumers to buy fewer imports and more nontradables within period 1, which requires p_{n1} (and therefore q) to rise to ensure market clearing. This is the intratemporal substitution effect whose magnitude is governed by the parameter ε, the intratemporal elasticity of substitution between nontradables and importables consumption. In addition, the rise in p_{m1} directly raises the consumption rate of interest (see equation 8), which causes substitution of aggregate consumption from period 1 to period 2, part of which falls on nontradable goods. This creates an incipient excess demand (supply) for future (current) period nontradables, the elimination of which requires a fall in q. The parameter governing this intertemporal substitution effect is σ, the intertemporal elasticity of substitution. If $\varepsilon > \sigma$, the intratemporal effect dominates the intertemporal effect and q rises in response to the temporary deterioration in the terms of trade, and vice versa if $\varepsilon < \sigma$. Substituting (9) into (8) gives

$$d \log R_c / d \log p_{m1} = -b\varepsilon / [b\varepsilon + (1 - b)\sigma]. \tag{8'}$$

Inspection of equation (8′) shows that the larger ε is, the larger is the increase in the consumption rate of interest in response to the terms-of-trade deterioration. The reason is that a large value of ε implies a large temporary appreciation of the real exchange rate (a large rise in q), which reinforces the direct effect of the terms-of-trade deterioration on the consumption rate of interest.

b. The real trade balance is given by

$$TA_c = (Y_{x1} - p_{m1} c_{m1})/P_1. \tag{10}$$

Totally differentiating equation (10) and taking into account the response of the real exchange rate gives

$$dTA_c / d \log p_{m1} = b\gamma C_1 \left[\frac{\sigma \varepsilon}{b\varepsilon + (1 - b)\sigma} - 1 \right]. \tag{11}$$

Equation (11) reveals that a temporary deterioration in the terms of trade may either improve or worsen the trade balance, depending on whether the expression before the minus sign is greater or less than unity (both cases are possible). It also reveals that, the larger either of the elasticities of substitution, σ or ε, the greater the improvement (the smaller the deterioration) in the trade balance as a result of a deterioration in the terms of trade. The intuition is that a relatively large value of ε implies a relatively large increase in the consumption interest rate in response to the terms-of-trade shock, since the real-exchange-rate ratio, q, rises by a relatively large amount. This tends to increase saving, and hence the trade balance, for a given value of the intertemporal elasticity of substitution. Further, for a given increase in the consumption rate of interest, the size of which depends positively on ε, saving rises by more as the intertemporal elasticity of substitution, σ, becomes larger. To sum up, therefore, relatively large values of ε or σ imply relatively large improvements (or relatively small deteriorations) in the trade balance in response to transitory adverse movements in the terms of trade.

Exercise V.11.4

Consider a two-period, two-country model with four goods: m (the home-country importable); x (the home-country exportable); n (the home-country nontradable); and n^* (the foreign-country nontradable). Agents in each country receive endowments of the two tradable goods as well as the country-specific nontradable good. They also consume the two tradable goods and the country-specific nontradable. There is perfect capital mobility.

Consider the effects on domestic and foreign consumption rates of interest of the imposition of a small temporary tariff by the home country, assuming lump-sum redistribution of the tariff revenue. In deriving your results, you may assume that preferences are identical in the two countries and are characterized by constant intratemporal elasticities of substitution (denoted ε) and intertemporal elasticities of substitution (denoted σ), and that the initial equilibrium is stationary so that expenditure shares are constant over time. You may also assume that the initial endowments and wealth levels are such that consumption interest rates and expenditure shares are equated across countries and, therefore, that transfer-problem criteria relating to cross-country differences in intratemporal or intertemporal spending propensities play no role in determining the effects of tariffs.

Solution

As usual, the solution to the comparative statics problem is derived by differentiating the equilibrium conditions. In this case, there are eight such conditions, one corresponding to each of the four goods in each of the two periods. Given that budget constraints hold, we can drop one such condition and work with the remaining seven, which allows us to find the effects of the temporary tariff on the seven prices in the system: the terms of trade in each period (two); the relative price of domestic nontradables in each period (two); the relative price of foreign nontradables in each period (two); and the world interest rate (one). The equilibrium conditions are provided here for convenience:

$$c_{x1}[p_{m1}(1 + \tau_1), p_{n1}, P_1 C_1(R_c, W_c)] + c_{x1}^*[p_{m1}, p_{n1}^*, P_1^* C_1^*(R_c^*, W_c^*)]$$

$$= Y_{x1} + Y_{x1}^*, \tag{1a}$$

$$c_{x2}[p_{m2}, p_{n2}, P_2 C_2(R_c, W_c)] + c_{x2}^*[p_{m2}, p_{n2}^*, P_2^* C_2^*(R_c^*, W_c^*)]$$

$$= Y_{x2} + Y_{x2}^*, \tag{1b}$$

$$c_{m1}[p_{m1}(1 + \tau_1), p_{n1}, P_1 C_1(R_c, W_c)] + c_{m1}^*[p_{m1}, p_{n1}^*, P_1^* C_1^*(R_c^*, W_c^*)]$$

$$= Y_{m1} + Y_{m1}^*, \tag{1c}$$

$$c_{m2}[p_{m2}, p_{n2}, P_2 C_2(R_c, W_c)] + c_{m2}^*[p_{m2}, p_{n2}^*, P_2^* C_2^*(R_c^*, W_c^*)]$$

$$= Y_{m2} + Y_{m2}^*, \tag{1d}$$

$$c_{n1}[p_{m1}(1 + \tau_1), p_{n1}, P_1 C_1(R_c, W_c)] = Y_{n1}, \tag{1e}$$

$$c_{n1}^*[p_{m1}, p_{n1}^*, P_1^* C_1^*(R_c^*, W_c^*)] = Y_{n1}^*, \tag{1f}$$

$$c_{n2}[p_{m2}, p_{n2}, P_2 C_2(R_c, W_c)] = Y_{n2}, \tag{1g}$$

$$c_{n2}^*[p_{m2}, p_{n2}^*, P_2^* C_2^*(R_c^*, W_c^*)] = Y_{n2}^*, \tag{1h}$$

where c_{it} denotes the demand for good $i = m, n, x$ in period $t = 1, 2$ and an asterisk denotes the foreign country's corresponding demand; relative prices are denoted in a similar manner with τ_1 representing the ad valorem tariff rate in period 1; $P_t(P_t^*)$ denotes the domestic (foreign) price index in period t and $C_t(C_t^*)$ denotes the domestic (foreign) real spending functions in period t; $R_c(R_c^*)$ denotes the domestic (foreign) consumption discount factor while $W_c(W_c^*)$ denotes domestic (foreign) consumption-based wealth, that is, wealth in terms of the numeraire deflated by the price index in period 1; and $Y_{it}(Y_{it}^*)$ denote domestic (foreign) endowments of good i in period t. Finally, wealth is in turn defined as the present value of current and future endowments evaluated using domestic prices and inclusive of rebated tariff revenue.

To find the effects on domestic and foreign consumption-based discount factors, we need to determine the effects on the world discount factor, R; on the terms-of-trade ratio, p_{m1}/p_{m2}; and on domestic and foreign real-exchange-rate ratios, p_{n1}/p_{n2} and p_{n1}^*/p_{n2}^*. Differentiating the equilibrium conditions (1a)–(1h) gives

$$d\log R/d\tau_1 = 0, \tag{2a}$$

$$d\log(p_{m1}/p_{m2})/d\tau_1 = -s, \tag{2b}$$

$$d\log(p_{n1}/p_{n2})/d\tau_1 = (1-s)b(\varepsilon - \sigma)/[(1-a)\varepsilon + a\sigma], \tag{2c}$$

$$d\log(p_{n1}^*/p_{n2}^*)/d\tau_1 = -sb(\varepsilon - \sigma)/[(1-a)\varepsilon + a\sigma], \tag{2d}$$

where s denotes the home country's share of world wealth; b denotes the initial expenditure share on good m; and a denotes the initial expenditure share on good n. The above results show that the imposition of the tariff leads to an improvement in the terms of trade for the tariff-imposing country that depends on how large the country is in world markets (as measured by its share of world wealth, s).[4] Given the improvement in the terms of trade, the domestic relative price of importables rises less than in proportion to the tariff while the foreign price of good m falls (recall s is a positive fraction). The behavior of the domestic real-exchange-rate ratio, p_{n1}/p_{n2}, depends both on the behavior of the domestic importables price ratio, $p_{m1}(1 + \tau_1)/p_{m2}$ (which, we have seen, rises in response to the tariff), and on the relative magnitudes of the intratemporal and inter-temporal elasticities of substitution. If ε is larger than σ, the imposition of the tariff requires p_{n1}/p_{n2} to rise since the within-period substitution effect (which raises demand for nontradables in period 1) dominates the inter-temporal substitution effect (which lowers demand for all goods, including nontradables) in period 1. The converse is true if $\varepsilon < \sigma$. By contrast, since the foreign price ratio for good m, p_{m1}/p_{m2}, falls when the tariff is imposed, it is immediately obvious that the foreign real-exchange-rate ratio, p_{n1}^*/p_{n2}^*, must fall when $\varepsilon < \sigma$ and rise when $\varepsilon > \sigma$. To sum up, therefore, under the assumption of identical tastes, domestic and foreign real-exchange-rate ra-

---

4. The fact that the world interest rate is unaffected by the tariff depends critically on the assumption of identical tastes, which rules out transfer effects.

tios must move asymetrically in response to the imposition of a temporary tariff.

Substituting equations (2a)–(2d) into the total differential of the expressions for the domestic and foreign consumption discount factors gives

$$d \log R_c / d\tau_1 = -(1-s)b\varepsilon/[(1-a)\varepsilon + a\sigma], \tag{3a}$$

$$d \log R_c^* / d\tau_1 = sb\varepsilon/[(1-a)\varepsilon + a\sigma]. \tag{3b}$$

From equations (3a) and (3b), it is clear that domestic and foreign consumption rates of interest are negatively correlated in response to the imposition of the tariff. The reason is that the internal relative price of good m rises in the home country but falls in the foreign country. This raises the relative cost of current consumption in terms of future consumption in the home country (that is, raises the domestic consumption rate of interest), but lowers the foreign consumption rate of interest.[5] Movements in domestic and foreign real-exchange-rates (equations 2c and 2d) may either reinforce or mitigate the direct effect of the tariff on the consumption discount factors, depending on the relative magnitudes of the intratemporal and intertemporal elasticities of substitution. However, under the assumption of identical *CES* utilities, real-exchange-rate effects cannot offset the direct effect of the tariff on the consumption discount factors.

References for Part V: [10], [12], [27], [32], [35], [41].

12

Capital Income Taxation in the Open Economy

Problems and solutions related to the material of this chapter of FR were covered under the heading for chapter 9.

---

5. A direct implication is that consumption growth rates, which do not depend on wealth under the assumption that preferences are homothetic, must move asymmetrically in response to the tariff.

VI

Stochastic Fiscal Policies

Exercise VI.13.1

Consider the infinite horizon model of a small open economy introduced in chapter 13, section 7. Assume that stochastic innovations (dz) of the returns (q_i) in risky assets are increments of a standard Wiener process (z):

$$q_i = \mu_i\, dt + \sigma_i\, dz_i, \qquad i = 1, 2, \ldots, n, \tag{1a}$$

so that asset i has mean μ_i and standard deviation σ_i. For simplicity, suppose that households receive no labor income. Also assume that the government follows a balanced-budget policy and taxes households in proportion to their beginning-of-period wealth and at a constant tax rate, τ. The stochastic innovations in τ are modelled as increments of a Wiener process with

$$\tau = \mu_g\, dt + \sigma_g\, dz_g. \tag{1b}$$

a. What determines a household's allocation of wealth among different risky assets? Are the optimal portfolio shares independent of a household's wealth? Show that if some risky assets had identical means and variances, domestic households would hold a larger share of the asset whose return has a higher covariance with government spending.

b. Assume domestic households have a power-utility function of the form

$$u(c) = (1/\eta)c^\eta, \quad \text{and} \quad 0 < \eta < 1. \tag{2}$$

Show that under the optimal consumption rule, if it exists, a household consumes a constant fraction of beginning-of-period wealth in each period. In this case, are the portfolio allocations independent of a household's wealth? What are the necessary transversality conditions for a well-defined solution? Suppose there is only one risky asset and define a countercyclical (procyclical) fiscal policy as one where, ceteris paribus, government spending is negatively (positively) correlated with asset returns. What are the effects of countercyclical and procyclical fiscal policies on the optimal consumption level?

Solution

a. The first part of this exercise asks us to assess characteristics of the optimal portfolio in a small open economy when investors have a choice among several risky assets. Without loss of generality, assume that there are two risky assets. In addition, there is one riskless asset offering a fixed return, r, per unit of time. The law of motion for financial assets over a discrete time interval Δt is described by

$$A_{t+\Delta t} = (A_t - c_t \Delta t)[(1 - \theta_1 - \theta_2)(1 + r\Delta t) + \theta_1(1 + q_{1t}\Delta t)$$
$$+ \theta_2(1 + q_{2t}\Delta t)] - A_t \tau_t \Delta t, \tag{3a}$$

where θ_i is the share of asset i in the household's portfolio. We assume that taxes are paid at the end of the period and in proportion to beginning-of-period wealth. Rewriting (3a) provides a convenient formula for the stochastic asset-accumulation path:

$$\Delta A_t = (A_t - c_t \Delta t)[(1 - \theta_1 - \theta_2)r + \theta_1 q_{1t} + \theta_2 q_{2t}]\Delta t - c_t \Delta t - A_t \tau_t \Delta t. \tag{3b}$$

With the underlying stochastic processes following a Brownian motion, one can use results from stochastic calculus to derive the first two moments of the law of motion for the change in wealth:

$$E\{dA_t\} = A_t[(1 - \theta_1 - \theta_2)r + \theta_1 \mu_1 + \theta_2 \mu_2]\,dt - c\,dt - A_t \mu_g \Delta t. \tag{4}$$

$$\text{Var}\{dA_t\} = A_t^2[\theta_1^2 \sigma_1^2 + \theta_2^2 \sigma_2^2 + 2\theta_1 \theta_2 \sigma_{12}) + \sigma_g^2 - 2\theta_1 \sigma_{g1} - 2\theta_2 \sigma_{g2}], \tag{5}$$

where σ_{ij} denotes the covariance of variables i and j. Using Ito's lemma to evaluate the value function, the Bellman equation for a consumer with a twice-differentiable and concave von Neumann-Morgenstern utility function is

$$\delta V = \max\{u(c) + V_A E\{dA\} + 1/2 V_{AA} \text{Var}\{dA\}\}, \tag{6}$$

where V is a function of wealth alone. Note that we do not need to be more specific about the utility function in this section. The maximization in equation (6) is with respect to consumption and the portfolio shares of each asset, given an initial wealth, A_0. To assess the optimal portfolio choice, insert the results from equations (4) and (5) into the consumer's decision problem and derive the first-order conditions with respect to the portfolio shares θ_i:[1]

$$\theta_1 = -\frac{1}{(\sigma_1^2\sigma_2^2 - \sigma_{12}^2)}\left\{\frac{V_A}{AV_{AA}}[(\mu_1 - r)\sigma_2^2 - (\mu_2 - r)\sigma_{12}]\right.$$

$$\left. + [\sigma_{g2}\sigma_{12} - \sigma_{g1}\sigma_2^2]\right\} \tag{7a}$$

$$\theta_2 = -\frac{1}{(\sigma_1^2\sigma_2^2 - \sigma_{12}^2)}\left\{\frac{V_A}{AV_{AA}}[(\mu_2 - r)\sigma_1^2 - (\mu_1 - r)\sigma_{12}]\right.$$

$$\left. + [\sigma_{g1}\sigma_{12} - \sigma_{g2}\sigma_1^2]\right\}. \tag{7b}$$

To analyze the optimal portfolio choice, consider first the allocation in the absence of stochastic government taxes. In this case, $\sigma_{gi} = 0$ and the share of each asset in the optimal portfolio is independent of a household's wealth: $\theta_i/\theta_j = $ constant. In the case of a closed economy, this corresponds to the result that all households hold the "market" portfolio. But once we introduce government taxes this result will not hold in general because taxes present a nondiversifiable risk. Instead, taxes are levied in proportion to the beginning-of-period asset position and are assessed irrespective of the payoffs during this particular time period. Under these conditions, additional restrictions on the household's preferences are needed (so that $V_A/(AV_{AA})$ is constant, see part b) for the optimal choice to involve constant portfolio shares across households of different wealth levels.

If assets were to offer the same mean return and had the same "riskiness" in terms of their variance, a consumer would generally hold a larger share in the asset whose covariance (σ_{gi}) is higher with respect to government taxes. From equations (7a) and (7b) we infer that if assets have the same mean return and variance, their relative portfolio shares are determined by the relative size of the covariances between the assets and government spending: If $\sigma_{g2} > \sigma_{g1}$, then $\theta_2 > \theta_1$, and vice versa. An asset that offers a relatively good insurance against a bad state, that is, a high payoff when taxes are high, is ceteris paribus preferred by the consumer.

b. More precise results can be obtained with additional restrictions on preferences. To derive the optimal consumption plan we assume that the

---

1. It is assumed that no short-sales restrictions apply.

consumer maximizes a power utility function with constant relative risk aversion $(1 - \eta)$. Without loss of generality, we will concentrate in this section on the case of a single risky asset in addition to the riskless bond.

The first-order condition for the optimal consumption choice is found by maximizing the Bellman equation (6) with respect to consumption:

$$c = V_A[1/(\eta - 1)]. \tag{8}$$

For the risky asset, the necessary condition is the analogue of equation (7), simplified for the case of a single risky asset:

$$\theta_1 = -\frac{V_A}{A V_{AA}}(\mu_1 - r) + \frac{\sigma_{g1}}{\sigma_1^2}. \tag{9}$$

The optimal consumption and portfolio choices can be substituted into the Bellman equation and we next "guess" a function, V, our candidate for solving this equation. Try $V(A) = MA^\eta$, where M is a constant, independent of wealth, if our guess is correct. To find M, we solve equation (6) using this functional form for $V(A)$ and the necessary conditions in equations (8) and (9). Rearranging terms gives the result:

$$\eta M = \left\{ \frac{1}{1 - \eta} \left\{ \delta - \eta r + \frac{\eta}{2(\eta - 1)} \frac{(\mu_1 - r)^2}{\sigma_1^2} + \eta\mu_g \right. \right.$$

$$\left. \left. - \eta\frac{\sigma_{g1}}{\sigma_1^2}(\mu_1 - r) + \eta(\eta - 1)\frac{1}{2\sigma_1^2}(\sigma_{g1}^2 - \sigma_g^2\sigma_1^2) \right\} \right\}^{(\eta-1)}$$

$$\equiv \phi_0^{\eta-1}. \tag{10}$$

As we had hoped, M is a constant independent of wealth. But for equation (10) to describe a legitimate solution, additional conditions will have to be satisfied. Essentially, these conditions rule out that the consumer can obtain infinite utility and that the optimal consumption rule is not unique. In particular, M must be positive for positive consumption levels; see equation (12) below. And the solution of equation (10) must be satisfied for a positive rate of time preference $(\delta > 0)$. Together, these two conditions give the following transversality condition:

$$\delta > \text{Max}\left\{ 0, \eta\left[r - \frac{1}{2(\eta - 1)}\left(\frac{\mu_1 - r}{\sigma_1} \right)^2 - \mu_g + \frac{\sigma_{g1}}{\sigma_1^2}(\mu_1 - r) \right. \right.$$

$$\left. \left. - (\eta - 1)\frac{1}{2\sigma_1^2}(\sigma_{g1}^2 - \sigma_1^2\sigma_g^2) \right] \right\}. \tag{11}$$

Equation (11) gives the stochastic analogue of the more familiar transversality condition in the growth literature that $\delta > \text{Max}\{0, \eta r\}$. If the condition is violated, the household can achieve infinite utility for any consumption plan with $c > 0$ if $\delta < 0$. And if $\delta > 0$ but equation (11) is still violated, the household can achieve infinite utility by saving its entire wealth ($\phi_0 = 0$ in this case and thus optimal consumption is also zero; see below).

Assuming that the transversality condition holds, we can determine the optimal consumption path from equations (8) and (10). Accordingly, households will consume a constant fraction of their wealth in each period:

$$c = \phi_0 A. \tag{12}$$

Regarding the allocation of wealth among different assets, it is straightforward to show that allocations are independent of a household's wealth level given our preference assumptions. This result also extends to the case of multiple risky assets. With only one risky asset, its share in the portfolio is determined from the optimal portfolio rule in equation (9) and the solution in equation (10):

$$\theta_1 = -\frac{\mu_1 - r}{\eta - 1} + \frac{\sigma_{g1}}{\sigma_1^2}. \tag{13}$$

Thus, if there is only one risky asset its share is directly proportional to its covariance with government taxes. If the asset pays relatively large returns in bad states, that is, states when government taxes are high, it provides a better insurance against adverse shocks than if it were to pay off relatively more in good states. Thus, the share of the risky asset is here an increasing function in its covariance with government taxes.

Finally, we study the response of the savings rate to changes in the stochastic path of government spending. We define the savings rate as the proportion of assets that is not consumed: $s = 1 - \phi_0$. Suppose that we isolate the effects of changes in government policies so that variations in one parameter (say the mean) would leave other parameters (for example, the variance) unchanged. First, consider the effects of a rise in the mean and the variance of government spending on the savings rate. By differentiating ϕ_0 in equation (10), we see that a rise in the mean would tend to lower the household's savings rate. But consumers would increase their savings rate to hedge against a greater riskiness of government taxation, with risk measured by the standard deviation of government taxes (σ_g).[2] The effects

---

2. It is well known that these results are specific to our assumptions with respect to preferences and the underlying stochastic processes.

on the savings rate of a procyclical government policy, one where government spending is positively correlated with the payoff of the risky asset, are ambiguous:

$$\frac{ds}{d\sigma_{g1}} = \frac{\eta}{1 - \eta} \frac{1}{\sigma_1^2} (\mu_1 - r) - \eta \frac{\sigma_{g1}}{\sigma_1^2}. \tag{14}$$

As a benchmark case, consider an initial state with "neutral" government policies ($\sigma_{g1} = 0$). The savings rate would increase if the government were to switch to a procyclical policy as long as the risky asset initially has a mean return in excess of the riskless asset. More generally, though, the savings rate can increase or decrease with variations in the government's interventionist policy stance.

Exercise VI.13.2

Consider a two-country, two-period stock market model. In the first period agents allocate their initial wealth among three assets: a riskless bond offering a return, R; a domestic equity offering an uncertain pretax return, R_1; and foreign equity with stochastic pretax return, R_2. Aside from the equity returns, domestic and foreign taxes form a second source of uncertainty. These are levelled on dividends from equity holdings in the second period with tax rates based on the country in which the equity was issued (source principle).

For simplicity, and unlike the model in chapter 13, suppose that consumption of a single consumer good is confined to the second period. Also assume that the agent's expected utility function can be represented by a mean-variance preference function:

$$E\{V_h\} - \frac{1}{2\tau_h} \text{Var}\{V_h\}, \tag{1}$$

where E denotes the expectation operator, Var the variance, and V_h is the home country's after-tax return on its portfolio. A similar function characterizes the foreign consumer's preferences. The parameter τ_j ($j = h, f$ and $\tau_j > 0$) may differ across countries and is a measure of the agent's risk tolerance, the marginal rate of substitution between variance and expected return.

a. Derive the necessary equilibrium conditions for the world stock market. Show that the after-tax excess returns can be described by a Capital Asset Pricing Model (CAPM) relationship.

b. Demonstrate that domestic and foreign agents will hold shares in the same world-market portfolio. Also prove that if domestic agents have a higher risk tolerance ($\tau_h > \tau_f$) and if the riskless asset is in zero net supply, the domestic agent will be a net borrower of the riskless asset.

c. Discuss how asset returns respond to changes in the stochastic properties of domestic taxes.

Solution

a. This exercise attempts to provide additional insights into the effects of government taxation on world stock markets. We begin by specifying the agent's decision problem and solve for the optimal portfolio allocation.

The representative agent's budget constraint implies that initial wealth is allocated among the three assets:

$$x_{0j} + x_{1j} + x_{2j} = 1, \qquad j = h, f. \tag{2}$$

In equation (2) x_{ij} indicates the share of initial wealth invested by the home (h) or foreign (f) country's consumer in each of the three assets; for example, x_{0h} denotes the proportion of initial wealth W_h that the home country invests in the riskless asset. The state-dependent portfolio return after tax and per unit of wealth is therefore

$$V_j = x_{0j}R + (1 - t_1)x_{1j}R_1 + (1 - t_2)x_{2j}R_2$$

$$\equiv x_{0j}R + x_{1j}R_{1t} + x_{2j}R_{2t}, \qquad j = h, f. \tag{3}$$

In equation (3), R_{it} denotes the after-tax return of asset i. Domestic and foreign agents have common beliefs about the stochastic processes and are not subject to any short-sales restrictions. Solving the objective function (1) for optimal portfolio shares subject to the budget constraint (2) yields the following necessary conditions:

$$E\{R_{1t}\} - \frac{1}{\tau_j}(x_{1j}\sigma_1^2 + x_{2j}\sigma_{12}) = \lambda_j \tag{4}$$

$$E\{R_{2t}\} - \frac{1}{\tau_j}(x_{2j}\sigma_2^2 + x_{1j}\sigma_{12}) = \lambda_j \qquad j = h, f. \tag{5}$$

$$R = \lambda_j, \tag{6}$$

where σ_{ik} denotes the after-tax covariance of assets i and k. Equations (4) and (5) describe the first-order condition for the optimal demand in domestic and foreign equity, respectively. Equation (6) indicates that the equilibrium return on the riskless asset equals the marginal utility of wealth for both the domestic and the foreign consumer.

To derive a *CAPM* relationship that connects the returns on individual assets with the return on the world-market portfolio we aggregate equations (4) to (6) across consumers. World equilibrium requires that the following three conditions are satisfied:

$$E\{R_{1t}\} - \frac{1}{\tau_w}(x_{1w}\sigma_1^2 + x_{2w}\sigma_{12}) = \lambda_w \tag{7}$$

$$E\{R_{2t}\} - \frac{1}{\tau_w}(x_{2w}\sigma_2^2 + x_{1w}\sigma_{12}) = \lambda_w \tag{8}$$

$$R = \lambda_w. \tag{9}$$

The world measure of risk tolerance (τ_w) is a wealth-weighted average of each country's risk tolerance ($\tau_w = [W_h/(W_h + W_f)]\tau_h + [W_f/(W_h + W_f)]\tau_f$). Similarly, the world marginal utility of wealth (λ_w) is a weighted average with the weights also depending on the countries' risk-tolerance measure: $\lambda_w = (1/\tau_w)(\tau_h[W_h/(W_h + W_f)]\lambda_h + \tau_f[W_f/(W_h + W_f)]\lambda_f)$. Equations (7) and (8) describe equilibrium returns of specific risky assets, but a similar relationship holds for any asset portfolio and in particular the world-market portfolio. Let σ_{iw} denote the covariance of the after-tax return of asset i with the world portfolio return, and let $\beta_{im} \equiv \sigma_{im}/\sigma_m^2$. Using the equilibrium relationship for the world-market portfolio and individual assets, and substituting for the marginal utility of wealth from equation (9) gives the equilibrium conditions for the excess returns on equities:

$$E\{R_{it}\} - R = [E\{R_{mt}\} - R]\beta_{im}, \qquad i = 1, 2. \tag{10}$$

The relationship described in equation (10) is the world-market analogue of the closed-economy *CAPM* and it incorporates the effects of country-specific taxation. The required payoff of an asset depends decisively on its covariance with the world-market portfolio return as captured by the parameter β_{im}. For example, if the home country's equity has an after-tax return that pays relatively high dividends in states where the world return is low, that is, if $\beta_{1m} < 0$, the domestic equity would require an after-tax return below the risk-free rate R. This asset itself would be risky, but the negative covariance of the asset reduces the aggregate variability of the investor's portfolio. Investors care about the variability of the overall portfolio and not about that of individual assets per se (see equation 1). An asset with a negative covariance would be comparatively good insurance against bad states, and its market can therefore clear even if the expected return is less than for the riskless asset.

b. In this part we are first asked to prove a two-fund separation theorem for the world stock market. The two funds are conveniently defined as consisting of a riskless asset and the world-market portfolio. To show that domestic and foreign agents will hold shares in the same portfolio we must demonstrate that the relative share of the two risky assets is the same for investors in both countries.

Substituting the riskless return for the marginal utility of wealth and combining the first-order conditions for the two equity instruments, one can derive the equilibrium condition for the relative investment shares:

$$\frac{x_{1j}}{x_{2j}} = \frac{1}{\frac{E\{R_{1t}\} - R}{E\{R_{2t}\} - R}\sigma_{12} - \sigma_1^2}\left(\sigma_{12} - \frac{E\{R_{1t}\} - R}{E\{R_{2t}\} - R}\sigma_2^2\right), \qquad j = h, f. \qquad (11)$$

The righthand side of equation (11) is independent of the country-specific preference parameters. Thus, domestic and foreign investors hold shares in the same portfolio, the world-market portfolio, even if they differ in their risk tolerance ($\tau_h \neq \tau_f$).

Different risk aversions will in general lead agents to hold different amounts of the second fund, that is, the riskless asset. To prove this point, combine equations (4) and (6) for the domestic and foreign agents. After rearranging terms, this yields

$$\tau_h = \frac{x_{1h}}{x_{1f}}\tau_f. \qquad (12)$$

A similar condition holds with respect to the second risky asset, the foreign equity claim. Therefore, if, for example, $\tau_h > \tau_f$, then $x_{1h} > x_{1f}$ and, similarly, $x_{2h} > x_{2f}$. It follows from the budget constraint that $x_{0h} < x_{0f}$. The intuition for the result is based on τ as a measure of risk aversion. If the domestic agent has a relatively high risk tolerance ($\tau_h > \tau_f$), then she will place a relatively small fraction of her wealth in the riskless asset. And although the relative share of different risky assets in the portfolio will be the same for investors in both countries (equation 11), the less risk-averse domestic investor would hold a larger portion of her assets in risky assets, and vice versa. A direct application of this result to the case where the riskless asset is in zero net supply is straightforward. Accordingly, the country whose relevant risk tolerance is lower will be a net holder of the riskless asset, and the second country is the corresponding net supplier.

c. The impact of government tax policies on asset valuations in the world stock market stems from two sources. First, a change in the mean tax rate has obvious implications for asset prices. From equation (10), an increase in the mean of domestic taxes would ceteris paribus require an increase in the relative pretax rate of return of the domestic equity; recall that the after-tax return, R_{1t}, is related to the pretax return, R_1, according to $E\{R_{1t}\} = E\{R_1\}(1 - E\{t_1\}) - \text{cov}(t_1, R_1)$. Secondly, stochastic government tax policies also affect asset prices through their second moments and in particular the covariance between taxes and returns of the market portfolio. For example, define a countercyclical (procyclical) tax policy as one where taxes are comparatively low (high) in bad states as measured by low returns in the world-market portfolio. Under otherwise unchanged conditions, including the same expected tax burden, a countercyclical tax policy implies a lower required rate of return on the domestic asset. It would allow a comparatively high after-tax return in bad states and reduce the variability of the private sector's total portfolio.

Exercise VI.13.3

Consider the two-country, two-period, open-economy model of chapter 13 in FR. Assume that there are two assets, a domestic and a foreign equity share, and that markets are complete.
a. Describe the government's optimal resource allocation across time and states if it maximizes a separable part of the private agent's expected utility function.
b. Assume that preferences of the representative domestic consumer can be described by the following expected utility function:

$$U = \frac{1}{1 - \sigma} [c_{h0}^{1-1/\sigma} + \delta \pi_0 c(0)_{h1}^{1-1/\sigma} + \delta \pi_1 c(1)_{h1}^{1-1/\sigma}] + U_g, \tag{1}$$

where U_g represents the utility derived from government consumption and π_s is the probability of state $s = 0, 1$. Assume that U_g and the representative foreign consumer's preferences are also described by power utility functions, although with possibly different substitution parameters σ, with $\sigma > 1$. Derive the optimal consumption plans for private agents and the government. Explain the implications for state-contingent prices of a redistribution of incomes from the private sector to the government.
c. Describe the effects of alternative tax paths across time and states on asset prices.

Solution

a. The government allocates a given level of resources, G, so as to maximizes U_g, the utility of its services to the private sector:

$$\max\{M(g_0) + \delta\pi_0 M(g_1[0]) + \delta\pi_1 M(g_1[1])\} \tag{2}$$

subject to: $g_0 + P_0 g_1(0) + P_1 g_1(1) = G,$

where P_s denotes the period 0 price of a unit of consumption in state s, and $M(\ )$ is the government's preference function. The government's choice variables are its levels of consumption in period 0, g_0, and in each of the two states in period 1, $g_1(s)$. Solving the decision problem in equation (2) and combining the first-order conditions for period 1 consumption yields

$$p = \frac{\pi_1 M'(g_1[1])}{\pi_0 M'(g_1[0])} \tag{3a}$$

$$P_s = \frac{\delta\pi_s M'(g_1[s])}{M'(g_0)}, \qquad s = 1, 2, \tag{3b}$$

with $p \equiv (P_1/P_0)$. According to equation (3a), the government will allocate its resources across different states to equalize the marginal rate of substitution and the relative price of state-contingent claims. Similarly, equation (3b) states that in equilibrium the marginal rate of substitution between current and future state-contingent consumption claims equals their relative price. These conditions correspond to familiar results for the private sector and will be used in the following analysis.

b. With complete markets we can consolidate the budget constraints for different periods and states into a single budget constraint. Accordingly, the sum of current and state-contingent future consumption claims cannot exceed the domestic private sector's initial wealth net of taxes:[3]

$$c_{h0} + P_0 c_{h1}(0) + P_1 c_{h1}(1) = W - G. \tag{4}$$

Maximizing the consumer's objective function (1) subject to the budget constraint (4) allows us to derive the demand equations for the domestic consumer:

---

3. The state-contingent claim prices can also be expressed in terms of the equity payoffs and equity prices discussed in chapter 13 of FR. Accordingly, $P_0 = (q/\theta_1(1) - q^*/\theta_1^*(1))/A$ and $P_1 = -P_0\theta_1^*(0)/\theta_1^*(1) + q^*/\theta_1^*(1)$, where $A \equiv \theta_1(0)/\theta_1(1) - \theta_1^*(0)/\theta_1^*(1)$. Here, $\theta_1(s)$ is the return of a domestic equity claim in state s of period 1 and q denotes the period 0 price of the domestic equity. A (*) indicates the corresponding variable related to the foreign equity.

$$c_{h0} = \frac{\delta^{-\sigma}}{\delta^{-\sigma} + P_0(P_0/\pi_0)^{-\sigma} + P_1(P_1/\pi_1)^{-\sigma}}(W - G) \qquad (5a)$$

$$c_{h1}(0) = \frac{(P_0/\pi_0)^{-\sigma}}{\delta^{-\sigma} + P_0(P_0/\pi_0)^{-\sigma} + P_1(P_1/\pi_1)^{-\sigma}}(W - G) \qquad (5b)$$

$$c_{h1}(1) = \frac{(P_1/\pi_1)^{-\sigma}}{\delta^{-\sigma} + P_0(P_0/\pi_0)^{-\sigma} + P_1(P_1/\pi_1)^{-\sigma}}(W - G). \qquad (5c)$$

Consumption in each period and state is proportional to initial net wealth with the factor of proportionality depending on preference parameters, the probability of different states, and state-contingent prices. Since preferences are homothetic, marginal and average propensities to consume are identical. It follows that the ratio of marginal propensities to consume in different states is independent of wealth:

$$\frac{MPC_{h1}(1)}{MPC_{h1}(0)} = \left[\frac{1}{p}\frac{\pi_1}{\pi_0}\right]^{\sigma}, \qquad (6)$$

where $MPC_{h1}(s)$ denotes the home country's marginal propensity to consume in state s; that is, $dc_{h1}(s)/d(W - G)$. The ratio of the marginal propensity to consume in different states is a function of three variables: the relative price of consumption in the two periods, the relative probability of the two states, and the substitution parameter σ. The relative marginal propensity to consume in state s is decreasing in the relative price of consumption in state s, reflecting the dominant substitution effect. An increase in the relative probability with which a state occurs would lead agents to allocate more resources to this state at the margin. The relative marginal propensity to consume is thus an increasing function of a state's relative probability. Finally, the relative marginal propensity to consume in different states is rising or falling with respect to the preference parameter σ, depending on whether the term $(1/p \ \pi_1/\pi_0)$, a measure of relative output in the two states, is greater or less than 1.

To analyze the effects on state-contingent prices of a redistribution of income from the domestic private sector to the government we can use the results of part a. Accordingly, the government's demand functions are similar to the private consumer's functions with government resources, G, and its substitution parameter, σ_g, replacing the corresponding private parameters, $(W - G)$ and σ, respectively. It will be convenient to define a function Z of the relative demand in states 1 and 2:

$$Z = \frac{c_{h1}(1) + c_{f1}(1) + g_1(1)}{c_{h1}(0) + c_{f1}(0) + g_1(0)}. \tag{7}$$

From the previous discussions it follows that Z depends on the relative price p but also on G since the preference parameters may differ for private and government agents: $Z = Z(p, G; \cdot)$. To assess the effect of a rise in G on relative demand in the two states and thus on the relative price of state-contingent consumption claims, we differentiate Z with respect to G initially holding p constant. The sign of the derivative depends on the relative marginal propensities to spend in the two states:

$$\text{sign}\{dZ/dG\} = \text{sign}\left\{\frac{MPC_g(1) - MPC_h(1)}{V_1} - \frac{MPC_g(0) - MPC_h(0)}{V_0}\right\}$$

$$= \text{sign}\{dp/dG\}, \tag{8}$$

where $V_s \equiv c_{h1}(s) + c_{f1}(s) + g_1(s)$ denotes world aggregate demand in state s. The first part of equation (8) provides the condition under which a redistribution of income from households to the public sector would increase the relative demand for state 1 consumption, holding the relative price p constant. For example, consider the case where the world supply of goods is the same in both states, $V_1 = V_0$. A redistribution of income in favor of the public sector would increase the relative demand for state 1 goods if the government's propensity to consume in state 1 versus that in state 0 is higher than the private sector's. Since the world supply of goods is given in both states and independent of the government's policy, a relative excess demand of state 1 goods must lead to an increase in the relative price of state 1 consumption. A rise in p would lower the relative demand for consumption in state 1 (compare equation 6) and contribute to the return of goods-market equilibrium. Similar arguments apply to an increase in government resources and its effect on the relative price of period 0 consumption and state-contingent prices, P_0 and P_1.

As discussed in chapter 13 of FR, a direct relationship exists between equity prices and state-contingent consumption prices. It is therefore straightforward and left to employ the above results and derive the implications for relative asset prices of a change in government spending.

c. Shifts in taxes across time and states have no impact on asset prices and demand allocations as long as the total value of resources used by the government, G, remains unchanged. Recall that $G = T_0 + P_0 T_1(0) + P_1 T_1(1)$. Since taxes are lump-sum, a shift, for example, from taxes in period 1 to taxes in period 0 would leave the complete market equilibrium unchanged around an initially balanced budget if $dT_0/dT_1(s) = -P_s$. Note that with complete markets, it is sufficient that this condition holds for a particular state s as long as G remains unchanged. On the other hand, if markets were incomplete a tax cut in period 0 would require appropriate tax increases in every state s. The stochastic Ricardian neutrality of government financing in the present model is therefore due to both the lump-sum nature of taxes and the complete market setup. Essentially, the government can apply the receipts from higher taxes in period 0 to buy state-contingent claims whose return in period 1 will exactly offset the cut in future taxes.

References for Part VI: [1], [24], [26], [27], [29].

Selected References

[1] Arnold, Ludwig. 1974. *Stochastic Differential Equations: Theory and Applications*. New York: Wiley.

[2] Blanchard, Olivier J. 1985. Debt, Deficits, and Finite Horizons. *Journal of Political Economy* 89:223–247.

[3] Buiter, Willem. 1988. Death, Birth, Productivity Growth and Debt Neutrality. *The Economic Journal* 98:279–293.

[4] Buiter, Willem. 1988. Structural and Stabilization Aspects of Fiscal and Financial Policy in the Dependent Economy. *Oxford Economic Papers* 40:220–245.

[5] Calvo, Guillermo A. 1987. On the Costs of Temporary Policy. *Journal of Development Economics* 27:245–261.

[6] Calvo, Guillermo A. 1988. Costly Trade Liberalizations: Durable Goods and Capital Mobility. *IMF Staff Papers* 35:461–473.

[7] Calvo, Guillermo A. 1989. Incredible Reforms. In *Debt, Stabilization and Development*, edited by Guillermo A. Calvo and others. Oxford: Blackwell.

[8] Devereux, Michael. 1987. Fiscal Spending, the Terms of Trade, and Real Interest Rates. *Journal of International Economics* 22:219–236.

[9] Devereux, Michael. 1988. Non-Traded Goods and the International Transmission of Fiscal Policy. *Canadian Journal of Economics* 21:265–278.

[10] Dixit, Avinash. 1985. Tax Policy in Open Economies. In Alan J. Auerbach and Martin Feldstein, eds., *Handbook of Public Economics*, vol. 1, 313–374.

[11] Djajic, Slobodan. 1987a. Effects of Budgetary Policies in Open Economies: The Role of Intertemporal Consumption Substitution. *Journal of International Money and Finance* 6:373–383.

[12] Djajic, Slobodan. 1987b. Temporary Import Quota and the Current Account. *Journal of International Economics* 22:349–362.

[13] Dornbusch, Rudiger. 1983. Real Interest Rates, Home Goods, and Optimal External Borrowing. *Journal of Political Economy* 91:141–153.

[14] Edwards, Sebastian. 1989. *Real Exchange Rates, Devaluations and Adjustment.* Cambridge: MIT Press.

[15] Edwards, Sebastian, and Ostry, Jonathan D. 1990. Anticipated Protectionist Policies, Real Exchange Rates and the Current Account. *Journal of International Money and Finance* 9:206–219.

[16] Edwards, Sebastian, and Ostry, Jonathan D. 1992. Terms of Trade Disturbances, Real Exchange Rates, and Welfare: The Role of Capital Controls and Labor Market Distortions. *Oxford Economic Papers* 44:20–34.

[17] Engel, Charles, and Kletzer, Kenneth. 1990. Tariffs and Saving in a Model with New Generations. *Journal of International Economics* 28:71–91.

[18] Frenkel, Jacob, and Razin, Assaf. 1987a. The Mundell-Flemming Model a Quarter Century Later: A Unified Exposition. *IMF Staff Papers* 34:567–620.

[19] Frenkel, Jacob, and Razin, Assaf. 1987b. *Fiscal Policies and the World Economy. An Intertemporal Approach.* Cambridge: MIT Press.

[20] Frenkel, Jacob, and Razin, Assaf. 1992. *Fiscal Policies and the World Economy: An Intertemporal Approach,* 2d ed. Cambridge: MIT Press.

[21] Froot, Kenneth A. 1988. Credibility, Real Interest Rates, and the Optimal Speed of Trade Liberalization. *Journal of International Economics* 25:71–93.

[22] Gardner, Grant W., and Kimbrough, Kent P. 1989. Tariffs, Interest Rates, and the Trade Balance in the World Economy. *Journal of International Economics* 27:91–110.

[23] Ghosh, Afish R., and Ostry, Jonathan D. 1992. Macroeconomic Uncertainty, Precautionary Savings and the Current Account. *IMF Working Paper* WP/92/72.

[24] Helpman, Elhanan, and Razin, Assaf. 1978. *A Theory of International Trade Under Uncertainty.* New York: Academic Press.

[25] Helpman, Elhanan, and Razin, Assaf. 1987. Exchange Rate Management: Intertemporal Tradeoffs. *American Economic Review* 77:107–123.

[26] Ingersoll, Jonathan E. Jr. 1987. *Theory of Financial Decision Making.* Totowa, NJ: Rowman & Littlefield.

[27] Levy, H., and Markowitz, H. 1979. Approximating Expected Utility by a Function of Mean and Variance. *American Economic Review* 69:308–317.

[28] Lopez, Ramon, and Rodrik, Dani. 1990. Trade Restrictions with Imported Intermediate Inputs: When Does the Trade Balance Improve? *Journal of Development Economics* 34:329–338.

[29] Lucas, Robert E. Jr. 1978. Asset Prices in an Exchange Economy. *Econometrica* 46:1429–1445.

[30] Marion, Nancy P. 1984. Nontraded Goods, Oil Price Increases, and the Current Account. *Journal of International Economics* 16:29–44.

[31] Murphy, Robert G. 1986. Tariffs, Non-Traded Goods and Fiscal Policy. *The International Trade Journal* 1:193–211.

[32] Ostry, Jonathan D. 1988. The Balance of Trade, Terms of Trade, and Real Exchange Rate: An Intertemporal Optimizing Framework. *IMF Staff Papers* 35: 541–573.

[33] Ostry, Jonathan D. 1989. Government Purchases and Relative Prices in a Two-Country World. *IMF Working Paper* WP/89/28.

[34] Ostry, Jonathan D. 1990. Tariffs and the Current Account: The Role of Initial Distortions. *Canadian Journal of Economics* 23:348–356.

[35] Ostry, Jonathan D. 1991a. Tariffs, Real Exchange Rates, and the Trade Balance in a Two-Country World. *European Economic Review* 35:1127–1142.

[36] Ostry, Jonathan D. 1991b. Trade Liberalization in Developing Countries: Initial Trade Distortions and Imported Intermediate Inputs. *IMF Staff Papers* 38: 447–479.

[37] Ostry, Jonathan D. 1992a. Trade Restrictions with Imported Intermediate Inputs: A Comment. *Journal of Development Economics* 38:403–405.

[38] Ostry, Jonathan D., and Reinhart, Carmen M. 1992. Private Saving and Terms of Trade Shocks: Evidence from Developing Countries. *IMF Staff Papers* 39:495–517.

[39] Ostry, Jonathan D., and Rose, Andrew K. 1992. An Empirical Evaluation of the Macroeconomic Effects of Tariffs. *Journal of International Money and Finance* 11:63–79.

[40] Razin, Assaf. 1984. Capital Movements, Intersectoral Resource Shifts and the Trade Balance. *European Economic Review* 26:135–152.

[41] Razin, Assaf, and Sadka, Efraim. 1991. Efficient Investment Incentives in the Presence of Capital Flight. *Journal of International Economics* 31:171–181.

[42] Razin, Assaf, and Svensson, Lars E. O. 1983. Trade Taxes and the Current Account. *Economics Letters* 13:55–57.

[43] Rodrik, Dani. 1987. Trade and Capital Account Liberalization in a Keynesian Economy. *Journal of International Economics* 23:113–129.

[44] Rodrik, Dani. 1989. Promises, Promises: Credible Policy Reform via Signalling. *Economic Journal* 99:756–772.

[45] Sharpe, William F. 1991. Capital Asset Prices with and without Negative Holdings. *Journal of Finance* 66:489–509.

[46] Svensson, Lars E. O. 1984. Oil Prices, Welfare and the Trade Balance. *Quarterly Journal of Economics* 94:649–672.

[47] Svensson, Lars E. O., and Razin, Assaf. 1983. The Terms of Trade and the Current Account: The Harberger-Laursen-Metzler Effect. *Journal of Political Economy* 91:97–125.

[48] van Wijnbergen, Sweder. 1987. Tariffs, Employment and the Current Account: Real Wage Resistance and the Macroeconomics of Protectionism. *International Economic Review* 28:691–706.

[49] Weil, Philippe. 1989. Overlapping Families of Infinitely Lived Agents. *Journal of Public Economics* 38:183–198.